THE DEVOTIONAL BIBLE STUDY NOTEBOOK

Also By Catherine Martin

Six Secrets to a Powerful Quiet Time
Knowing and Loving the Bible
Walking with the God Who Cares
Set my Heart on Fire
Trusting in the Names of God
Passionate Prayer
A Heart That Hopes in God
Run Before the Wind
Trusting in the Names of God—A Quiet Time Experience
Passionate Prayer—A Quiet Time Experience
Pilgrimage of the Heart
Revive My Heart
A Heart That Dances
A Heart on Fire
A Heart to See Forever
Quiet Time Moments for Women
Drawing Strength from the Names of God
A Woman's Heart that Dances
A Woman's Walk in Grace
The Quiet Time Journal
The Quiet Time Notebook
The Passionate Prayer Notebook

Catherine Martin

The Devotional Bible Study Notebook

PALM DESERT, CALIFORNIA

Cover by Quiet Time Ministries.
Cover photo by Catherine Martin—myPhotoWalk.com

The Devotional Bible Study Notebook

Published by Quiet Time Ministries
Palm Desert, California 92255
www.quiettime.org

ISBN-13: 978-0-9766886-7-9

Second Edition published by Quiet Time Ministries 2013

Printed in the United States of America
13 14 15 16 17 18 19 20 21/ LSI /11 10 9 8 7 6 5 4 3 2

EX LIBRIS

____

Dates

____

____

My Key Word & Verse

____

____

Your word is a lamp to my feet and a light to my path.

PSALM 119:105

Let the word of Christ richly dwell within you,
teaching and admonishing one another
with psalms and hymns and spiritual songs,
singing with thankfulness
in your hearts to God.

COLOSSIANS 3:16

The Bible you hold in your hands is an incredible treasure.
In the Bible God is telling you what is on His mind
and in His heart. It is His love letter to you.
It is a handbook for your life. It is the ultimate
how-to book. God is speaking to you personally
in the Bible... The Bible is not merely static words
on a page but the living Word of God.

CATHERINE MARTIN, KNOWING AND LOVING THE BIBLE

CONTENTS

INTRODUCTION

I remember the first time I traveled to Florence, Italy, one of my very favorite places in all the world. I could have explored the streets of that city for a year and still not exhausted all the amazing facets of its beauty. I think about the day my husband and I were roaming the streets, took a turn down an alley, and then walked through the doors of the Church at Santa Croce. What we saw took our breath away. In that one church we found the tombs of Machiavelli, Dante, and Michelangelo. The marble floors were artistic and beautiful; the wood ceiling was carved intricately with magnificence. We sat in one of the pews and just drank in the atmosphere of that place. And then, another day we took a bus to Fiesole, a small town above Florence. From Fiesole, high above Florence, we could see the city from a completely different perspective. Red tile roofs glistened in the sun and made the city appear as a jewel in the midst of the green rolling hills of Tuscany.

Opening the pages of God's Word is very much like the experience of visiting unknown lands where every day is filled with new discoveries. To get the most from God's Word, we need to spend time getting the big view and then zooming to explore every nook and cranny of it. Paul encourages extravagance with God's Word when he writes, "Let the word of Christ richly dwell within you, with all wisdom teaching and admonishing one another with psalms and hymns and spiritual songs, singing with thankfulness in your hearts to God" (Colossians 3:16). When you live in God's Word, it will begin to live in you, and you will experience a firm foundation in life and your faith will grow.

I remember as a new Christian, I visited the local Christian bookstore to buy a Bible. After looking at all the different translations and types of Bibles, I finally sought the help of the bookstore owner. I remember how she opened the Bible to show me the pages. You could smell the newness of the paper and the leather of the binding. She taught me how to open the pages of a new Bible, a section at a time, to break it in. I remember walking out of the bookstore, holding the Bible close, excited at the prospect of knowing God and hearing what He had to say to me.

But I admit, I didn't become a student of God's Word overnight. In fact, at first, I had no idea where to begin. I read a little bit here and a little bit there, and only barely understanding the words. I always read with a pencil in my hand to underline favorite verses and easily find them again. Within a few months, I discovered some verses that I absolutely loved.

"Delight yourself in the LORD and He will give you the desires of your heart" (Psalm 37:4).

"And we know that God causes all things to work together for good to those who love God, to those who are called according to His purpose" (Romans 8:28).

"Draw near to God and He will draw near to you" (James 4:8).

"Cease striving and know that I am God; I will be exalted among the nations, I will be exalted in the earth" (Psalm 46:10).

"Thus says the LORD, 'Let not a wise man boast of his wisdom, and let not the mighty man boast of his might, let not a rich man boast of his riches; but let him who boasts boast of this, that he understands and knows Me, that I am the LORD who exercises lovingkindness, justice and righteousness on earth; for I delight in these things,' declares the LORD" (Jeremiah 9:23-24).

All these verses became embedded in my heart. I returned to them again and again. I remember feeling compelled to write out what God was teaching me. So I got a notebook with lined paper where I could write my insights as I read different verses in the Bible.

I became much more serious about my time in God's Word after reading three important books. First, I read *The Pursuit of God* by A.W. Tozer. In that book, Tozer said, "Sound Bible exposition is an imperative *must* in the Church of the Living God…it is not mere words that nourish the soul, but God Himself, and unless and until the hearers find God in personal experience they are not the better for having heard the truth. The Bible is not an end in itself, but a means to bring men to an intimate and satisfying knowledge of God, that they may enter into Him, that they may delight in His Presence, may taste and know the inner sweetness of the very God Himself in the core and center of their hearts."[1] I wrote next to those words in the margin of my first copy of Tozer's book, "Purpose of the Word." His words resonated with the very desire in my heart brought about my first early reading of the Bible. I found a deep hunger for God and desire to know Him more growing with each day I spent in His Word. My desire to know God was named and described as "the pursuit of God" by Tozer.

The second important book for me was *Knowing God* by J.I. Packer. I read that pivotal book with a friend, Kathy Cottrell, and together we shared the significant truths and insights gleaned from that book. I think sharing the book with Kathy was an imperative part of my own journey, because talking through those truths cemented them in my heart. The great, life-changing words for me in *Knowing God* were at the beginning of chapter 3. Packer writes, "What were we made for? To know God. What aim should we set ourselves in life? To know God. What is the 'eternal life' that Jesus gives? Knowledge of God. 'This is life eternal, that they might know thee, the only true God, and Jesus Christ, whom thou hast sent' (John 17:3). What is the best thing in life, bringing more joy, delight, and contentment, than anything else? Knowledge of God."[2] When I read those words, I determined that my priorities, affections, and goals needed to shift to one primary pursuit: knowing God.

Then I discovered my life verse, Psalm 27:4, written by David, the man after God's own heart. He wrote, "One thing I have asked from the LORD, that I shall seek; that I may dwell in the house of the LORD all the days of my life, to behold the beauty of the LORD and to meditate in His temple." In these words I realized I would need to set aside many things in order to pursue this one great desire of knowing God. Knowing Him became more important to me than becoming wealthy, having a good job, or achieving any kind of earthly success.

The third important book I read during this time was *Faith Is Not A Feeling* by Ney Bailey. I loved this book with its practical stories and teaching on faith. But Ney Bailey's definition of faith, in all its simplicity, changed my life and filled me with a great passion to know and love the Bible. She arrived at her definition of faith through the story in Luke 7:1-10. The centurion wanted Jesus to heal his slave, who was sick and about to die. He sent some Jewish elders to Jesus, asking him to come and save the life of his slave. But then, while Jesus was on his way, the centurion sent a message, saying he was unworthy to have Jesus in his house. He said, "Just say the word, and my servant will be healed" (Luke 7:7). Jesus marveled at him, and turned to the crowd, and said, "I say to you, not even in Israel have I found such great faith" (Luke 7:9). Jesus then healed the centurion's slave. Ney Bailey made her own great discovery in the Bible, and defined faith as *taking God at His Word.*

When I read that definition, I felt as though a huge light of truth came on for me. How could I become a woman of faith unless I knew God's Word? I realized my faith would grow to the degree that I knew God's Word. I could know God more if I opened the pages of His Word. To me, I saw the Word of God as a key that would unlock the door to my own personal experience of knowing God and becoming a woman who walked by faith.

So my time in God's Word took on a whole new purpose and dimension, as I endeavored to know God and grow in my faith. My notebook became much more important as a companion to my quiet time in God's Word. I used my notebook for Bible study, writing out my observations, writing out different translations of great verses, recording quotes from commentaries and books, and keeping track of verses that truths related to topics or characters in the Bible.

I want to ask you, "Have you discovered the great adventure of knowing God in His Word? Would you like to grow in your love for God and His Word? Do you want to become and man or woman who walks by faith, not by sight? I want to invite you to discover the excitement and adventure of studying God's Word with the goal of knowing and loving God, and glorifying Him with your very life.

You hold in your hands some of the fruit of all my years of study in God's Word, *The Devotional Bible Study Notebook.* Over the years, I've learned many different kinds of studies in God's Word, drawing me deeper into His Presence, and teaching me more and more how to live by faith. I've always regarded Bible study as somewhat of an experiment, in that some things seemed to work most effectively in helping me know and understand what God was saying to me in His Word.

The *Devotional Bible Study Notebook* contains pages for the studies in God's Word that I love the most and have found to be especially effective and life-changing. These studies include:

- Observation Study
- Translation Study
- Verse Study
- Word Study
- Reference or Topical Study
- Character Study
- Doctrine or Ethics Study

These pages can be used in many ways as you open the pages of your Bible. They are a place for you to write out what God teaches you. There is space for you to write insights, observations, thoughts, prayers, and any other practical applications that God works into your life from your time in His Word.

I've excerpted chapters from my book, *Knowing and Loving the Bible*, to help get you started in studying God's Word more in your quiet time using *The Devotional Bible Study Notebook*. The exciting part is that not only will you read about how to study God's Word, you have a resource that will help you immediately apply what you learn in Bible study.

The Devotional Bible Study Notebook is designed to be a resource for you in your quiet time. And when its pages are filled, you will have a testimony in written form of all that God is teaching you in His Word. You will notice there is a place at the front of *The Devotional Bible Study Notebook* for you to write your name, the dates, and a key verse. You may use more than one *Devotional Bible Study Notebooks* in a year, and they will be chronicles of your adventure with the Lord as you grow in your knowledge of Him.

So dear friend, will you set aside the many things for the one thing in life, the great pursuit of knowing God? Someday you will stand face to face with your Lord. I want you to be able to look into eyes that are familiar to you because you have spent much time with Him now. I want you to enjoy His beauty and experience His love. When you are face to face with Him, you will know that your time alone with Him in His Word was worth it all. God bless you, dear friend, as you engage in the great adventure of knowing Him.

Quiet Time Ministries Online

Quiet Time Ministries Online at www.quiettime.org is a place where you can deepen your devotion to God and His Word. Cath's Blog is where Catherine shares about life, about the Lord, and just about everything else. A Walk In Grace™ is Catherine's devotional photojournal, highlighting her own photography, where you can grow deep in the garden of His grace. Quiet Time Ministries proudly sponsors Ministry For Women at www.ministryforwomen.com—a social network community for women worldwide to grow in their relationship with Jesus Christ. Connect, study, and grow at Ministry For Women. Quiet Time Ministries proudly sponsors Catherine Martin's myPhotoWalk at www.myphotowalk.com where lovers of photography can experience the great adventure of knowing God through Devotional Photography.

My Letter To The Lord

As you begin using *The Devotional Bible Study Notebook*, I'd like to ask, where are you? What has been happening in your life over the last year or so? What has been your life experience? What are you facing and what has God been teaching you? It is no accident that you have *The Devotional Bible Study Notebook* to use in your quiet time. In fact, God has something He wants you to know, something that will change the whole landscape of your experience with Him. Watch for it, listen for it, and when you learn it, write it down and never let it go. Will you write a prayer in the form of a letter to the Lord in the space provided expressing all that is on your heart and ask Him to speak to you as you draw near and grow in your quiet time with Him?

My Letter To The Lord

THE DEVOTIONAL BIBLE STUDY GUIDE

Chapter 1

THE TREASURE OF GOD'S WORD

But know this first of all, that no prophecy of Scripture is a matter of one's own interpretation, for no prophecy was ever made by an act of human will, but men moved by the Holy Spirit spoke from God.
2 Peter 1:20-21

The Bible you hold in your hands is an incredible treasure. In the Bible God is telling you what is on His mind and in His heart. It is His love letter to you. It is a handbook for your life. It is the ultimate how-to book. God is speaking to you personally in the Bible. Peter has made this clear in 2 Peter 1:20-21: "But know this first of all, that no prophecy of Scripture is a matter of one's own interpretation, for no prophecy was ever made by an act of human will, but men moved by the Holy Spirit spoke from God." The Bible is not merely static words on a page but the living Word of God.

I remember one day many years ago talking with a friend about the Bible. I had been in seminary for at least a year and was so excited at what I was learning about the origin of the Bible. I told my friend about the journeys of Paul, his imprisonment, and his great love for the church as a background for his biblical letters. As I spoke, I saw a look of shock on her face, and I asked what was wrong. She replied, "Are you telling me that a real person actually wrote the words of Paul's letters?" I explained that it was God's Word, inspired by Him, but written through Paul in a real historical context. Then I asked her how she thought the Bible had been written. She thought the Bible had just appeared out of nowhere, mystically, without the involvement of human personality at all.

What is your concept of the Bible? Do you know what you hold in your hands when you open the pages of God's Word? A spiritual battle is being waged throughout the world for the truth of the Word of God. There are special interest, academic, and political groups tearing the Bible apart. When they have completed their work, they will have nothing of substance remaining. Some groups are eliminating the miraculous, denying the power and authority of God. Others are adding to the Bible in order to promote their own agendas, thoughts, and beliefs. Still others are choosing to give precedence to extrabiblical texts rather than the Bible. The battle over what constitutes the Word of God began in the early church, escalated during the Reformation, and is accelerating in the present age. In fact, countless people have sacrificed their lives that we might have a Bible in our hands so we might draw near to know and love God.

The Uniqueness of the Bible

There is a reason why the Bible is the bestseller of all time. There is a reason why Bibles are marked up by men and women who have walked with God throughout their lives. There is a reason why Corrie ten Boom made every effort to carry her Bible with her into the horror of Ravensbruck concentration camp. There is a reason why a believing prison guard gave Bibles to every prisoner, knowing they were about to die. The Bible is more than a book. It is unique for several reasons.

The Bible has the power to change your life. Howard Hendricks says, "The Bible was written not to satisfy your curiosity but to help you conform to Christ's image. Not to make you a smarter sinner but to make you like the Savior. Not to fill your head with a collection of biblical facts but to transform your life."[1] The very deepest parts of our being are probed with the Great Physician's scalpel, yielding a perspective no human insight can provide. The Bible changes your life and does for you what you cannot do for yourself. "For the word of God is living and active and sharper than any two-edged sword, and piercing as far as the division of soul and spirit, of both joints and marrow, and able to judge the thoughts and intentions of the heart" (Hebrews 4:12).

The Bible is the revelation of God. When you open your Bible you will discover 66 books written over 1500 years of history by at least 40 authors. In other words, God revealed Himself and His ways to man progressively over a period of time. "God, after He spoke long ago to the fathers in the prophets in many portions and in many ways, in these last days has spoken to us in His Son" (Hebrews 1:1-2).

The Bible, God's Word, is written in a known human language. God chose to speak in language that human beings could understand. The original language of the Old Testament is ancient Hebrew with some Aramaic, and the original language of the New Testament is Koine Greek (the common language of the people in the first century) with some Aramaic phrases. Because the Bible was written in known languages, it could be translated into multitudes of other languages. In fact, it is being translated into new languages even at this very hour by skilled translators so that it may be read by people throughout the world. Glen C. Scorgie, in the book *The Challenge of Bible Translation*, helps us to not take this for granted:

> The divinely inspired Word first communicated through Hebrew and Greek language (and the ways of viewing life that those languages reflected) can now

> be meaningfully conveyed through other human languages as well. It is a great grace—and one to be celebrated by Christians—that divinely revealed truth is portable between linguistic systems and equally potent in its new dress.[2]

The Bible has a background and context in history. The revelation of God is given within a historical context; that is, God sent His message through many authors, each with his own personality, expressing his own cultural background. J. Robertson McQuilken makes this note in his book *Understanding and Applying the Bible*:

> The Bible is revelation in history, unlike the teachings of many religions. Some religions are rooted in mythology, such as Shintoism or Hinduism. Others were founded by a historic individual, but large elements of religious teachings today are mythological, such as Buddhism. In contrast to those, Scripture is rooted in history and claims to be a historical document, the record of God's self-revelation to man. As such, we must understand it in the context of its history.[3]

This historical context allows for an accurate study of cultures, historical events, and interpretation.

The Bible is written by God and inspired by God. Although it was written over a great time span by many authors, the Bible presents a distinct unity in thought and belief. The Bible is inspired by God. This means He is the author, the single source affirming the authenticity and trustworthiness of the entire biblical canon. Josh McDowell challenged a representative of *The Great Books of the Western World* to consider just ten authors, all from one walk of life, one generation, one place, one mood, and one language, and just one controversial subject. He then asked the representative, "Would the authors agree with one another?" The man admitted, "No." Josh then presented the uniformity of thought in the biblical text. Days later, the man committed his life to Christ.[4]

The Bible is unlike any other book. Imagine that God purposed in His heart and mind to give us something tangible in a language we can understand so that we may know and love Him. It is a miracle that we can even have such a treasure. All earthly possessions erode over time, but not the Word of God. It is eternal.

The Bible Is Inspired

"All Scripture is inspired by God and profitable for teaching, for reproof, for correction, for training in righteousness; so that the man of God may be adequate, equipped for every good work" (2 Timothy 3:16). The Greek word for *inspired* is *theopneustos* and literally means "God-breathed," meaning that the origin is God, not man. The Holy Spirit so worked through the human writers, despite different styles and personalities, that the written Word of God is authoritative, trustworthy, and free from error in the original autographs.[5]

The Bible Is Inerrant

To say that the Bible is inerrant is to say that it tells the truth and is free from error. Different styles of writing and different views of the same event do not constitute error. Paul Enns says the following about inerrancy of Scripture:

> When correctly understood, it means that the Bible speaks accurately in all its statements, whether theological matters, the creation account, history, geography, or geology. It does, however, allow for variety in details concerning the same account; it does not demand rigidity of style. In all the Bible's statements it is accurate and in accord with the truth.[6]

The Bible Is Infallible

In the fall of 1978, an international summit conference of evangelical leaders produced the Chicago Statement on Biblical Inerrancy, which includes this sentence: "*Infallible* signifies the quality of neither mis-leading nor being misled and so safeguards in categorical terms the truth that Holy Scripture is a sure, safe, and reliable rule and guide in all matters."[7] It is dependable as the object of your faith and the sure foundation to give you confidence to do what it says.

Sola Scriptura

Sola scriptura implies that the Bible is the sole authority for one's belief. *Sola scriptura*, the Latin phrase meaning "Scripture alone," was coined by the theologians of the Reformation to point out that only the Bible has the right to command the beliefs and actions of people. It is the final court of appeals for all doctrine and practice, is infallible, and is all that is needed to know God's truth. This contrasts with the belief that an additional teaching authority such as the church, a religious guru, or a governing body is required to understand the Bible.

The principle of *sola scriptura* reached its zenith in the early sixteenth century as Martin Luther nailed his "95 Theses" to the church door at Wittenberg. Following a powerful spiritual experience centered on Romans 1:18, "the just shall live by faith," Luther held that the sole authority for Christian experience was the Word of God, in contrast to the teachings of the church of his day. Luther was arrested and brought before the authorities of the church, who demanded that he recant all his teachings. He prayed all night. When he returned, he spoke with such force and power about the truth of God's Word and the sole authority of God's Word that the room was silent. He said the following: "Unless I am convicted of error by the testimony of Scriptures or (since I put no trust in the unsupported authority of the Pope or of councils, since it is plain that they have erred and often contradicted themselves) by manifest reasoning I stand convicted by the Scriptures to which I have appealed, and my conscience is taken captive by God's word, I cannot and will not recant anything, for to act against conscience is neither safe for us nor open to us. On this I take my stand. I can do no other. God help me. Amen." Luther was not executed that day. The ongoing work of the Bible continued, and ultimately it made its way into the hands of the people.

The Canon

The word *canon,* when used in connection with the Bible, describes the collection of the 66 books comprising the inspired Word of God. It is the Bible as we know it today. Whereas the Greek origin is *kanon,* the Hebrew word is *qaneh,* the word for a measuring rod. The Council of Jamnia in ad 90 is generally considered the occasion when the Old Testament canon was publicly recognized. Criteria for the Old Testament canon included internal evidence of divine authorship, the writer as spokesman for God, and historical accuracy. The process of the recognition and collection of the New Testament canon took place in the first centuries of the Christian church. Criteria for the New Testament canon included apostolicity, acceptance, content, and inspiration. At no time were the councils causing inspiration; they were simply recognizing it. Therefore, the Bible you hold in your hands is complete and what God intended to say to you in written form. That is why it has often been called His love letter to you.

The Bible Is Reliable

The reliability of the Bible depends on its accuracy. As original manuscripts began to show wear over time, they were reverently copied by ancient scribes, word by word, character by character, to produce exact copies of each book of the Bible. From the days of Ezra, the tradition of copying text included quite tedious procedures, such as counting letters in a book and noting middle letters in the text. The discovery of the Dead Sea Scrolls in 1947 was the defining moment in modern history for substantiating biblical accuracy. From that archaeological find, the oldest manuscripts of the Bible could be compared to the subsequent manuscripts throughout history, thus confirming textual accuracy.

The History of the Printed Bible

Imagine a world without a written Bible. For many centuries, the Bible was only in the hands of the church leaders, its sole interpreters and dictators of the beliefs and actions of the people. How did the Bible move from ancient writing on papyrus to the printed word we have today? The word *Bible* comes from the Greek word *biblion*, which in turn comes from the word *biblos*, another word for the plant that is the source for papyrus, the writing material of the ancient world.[8] Other writing materials in the ancient world included parchment and leather. Because parchment was more durable than papyrus, most of our Old Testament and New Testament manuscripts are parchment. The originals were most likely written on papyrus (see 2 John 12).

Throughout the centuries, various translators took the available collections of the Old and New Testaments and translated them into the languages of the day. One of the earliest translations was the Latin Vulgate by Jerome in the fourth century. Not until Gutenberg published the first Bible in 1452 were these translations duplicated and available to the masses. Gutenberg printed 30 copies on parchment using some 46,000 wood blocks of movable type. During the next 50 years, 100 editions of his two-volume Latin Bible were published. Erasmus published the first Greek New Testament with a definitive fourth edition in 1527.

With the Bible in Latin or Greek, the Word of God was not readily available to those who could read only English. Therefore, people relied on the church to interpret Scripture for them. Unfortunately, the church often served its own interests and created many religious ideas that did not have their origin in Scripture.

John Wycliffe, an Oxford theologian in the late 1300s, was burdened for people to have their own Bibles so that they might order their lives by the truth of its words. His passion was to give the people the Word of God in their own language. He developed an English version of the Bible translated directly from the Latin Vulgate, but this new translation was a direct threat to the church. In 1415, the Council of Constance condemned the writings of Wycliffe, and in 1428, his bones were dug up and burned.

William Tyndale (1494–1536) is considered to be the true father of the English Bible because his English translation was derived from the original Hebrew and Greek, and it was printed rather than copied.[9] Tyndale vowed that the plowboy would know more about Scripture than the priests. His desire was to promote Christian growth and effectiveness in the lives of all the people. We see this in his statement in the Old English style: "that the sainctes might have all thinges necessarie to worke and minister with all, to the edifyinge of the body of Christ."[10] Tyndale realized his dream of an English translation of the Bible by leaving his beloved country, England, and traveling to Germany to complete the work. Tyndale barely escaped from Cologne when his work became known and was forbidden by authorities. The first printing of his New Testament in

English was completed in Worms in 1526. Within a month, copies made their way to England, smuggled in barrels and other containers of merchandise. The church was incensed and burned as many copies as it could find. Tyndale continued his work of translation and printing until Emperor Charles V declared him a heretic and condemned him to be executed. William Tyndale was strangled to death and then burned at the stake in 1536. His last words were, "Lord, open the King of England's eyes."[11]

A Bible of Your Own

It is a wondrous privilege that you and I can have our own Bibles to open, read, and study whenever we choose. Thousands of Bibles are available in many languages throughout the world because of the sacrifice of such men as Luther, Wycliffe, and Tyndale. And now, think about your own Bible. You may have study Bibles, commentaries, and other resources to help you grow. However, the most important tool in your life is a Bible that you can read, live in, and grow to know and love. Choose a Bible that has an easily readable type and font size. Choose a soft leather edition if you can afford it. You will want a size that you can carry around. Have a good supply of pens and pencils to use for marking in your Bible. Then, get ready for the adventure of your life as you take advantage of the opportunity God has given to you through such servants as Tyndale and Wycliffe, and open the pages of your Bible.

The Treasure You Have In Your Hands

You may hardly be able to imagine that holding the Bible in your own hands was once considered a crime. But such was the case for people like Tyndale and Wycliffe. Could you imagine your church calling you in front of the board to ask you to lay aside the authority of God's Word in your life? But some forces in the world today would keep you from opening your Bible in public. Paul describes our spiritual battle in Ephesians 6:12-13:

> Our struggle is not against flesh and blood, but against the rulers, against the powers, against the world forces of this darkness, against the spiritual forces of wickedness in the heavenly places. Therefore, take up the full armor of God, so that you will be able to resist in the evil day, and having done everything, to stand firm.

Paul ends this section on spiritual warfare by telling you to take up the "sword of the Spirit, which is the word of God" (Ephesians 6:17). Oh, how desperately we need men and women who have hearts like Luther's and Tyndale's, spiritual warriors willing to stand against the tide and fight for the truth of God's Word! Think about the transmission of the texts down through the years and those who risked and actually gave their lives so that you might hold a Bible in your hands. It gives great cause for thanks to a gracious God, who would give such a gift to you. Now the question is, will you take advantage of the great opportunity to open the pages of His Word and hear what He has to say to you? If so, then you are God's man or God's woman for such a time as this.

CHAPTER 2

DISCOVERING SECRETS IN THE WORD

I will show you secrets you have never known.
ISAIAH 48:6 CEV

God wants to tell you His secrets. He says, "Pray to me and I will answer you. I will tell you important secrets you have never heard before" (Jeremiah 33:3 NCV). We learn from the psalmist in Psalm 25:14 (TLB), "Friendship with God is reserved for those who reverence Him. With them alone He shares the secrets of His promises." When you know people's secrets, they include you in their inner circle. God's inner circle is called "friendship with God." God says, "I will show you secrets you have never known" (Isaiah 48:6 CEV). These truths that God wants to show His people remain hidden if we neglect what He says in His Word. Most people are observers rather than participants with God. Many feel as though a great distance separates them from God. When one reads the Bible as unfamiliar territory without any knowledge of how to traverse it, this sense of distance grows. Wouldn't you rather be a friend of God than a stranger? Wouldn't you love to have Him tell you His secrets?

When my husband and I first moved to Palm Desert, California, I felt alone and disconnected from everything I knew and loved. I would drive down unfamiliar roads, take wrong turns, and end up in the strangest places. After a year of driving around the area, everything had become so familiar that I began to enjoy the beauty of my new desert surroundings. I found favorite stores, restaurants, and wonderful friends that added to that sense of familiarity. It became my home.

What will help you come to the place where the Bible becomes familiar territory with countless roads that take you straight to the heart of God? What will make the Bible a home to you? What will help you hear and see God's secrets in His Word? Adding devotional Bible study to your quiet time. What this will mean for you, practically speaking, is that you will sit with the Bible for a few extra moments in your quiet time and think more deeply about what it says as you are reading. It means you will take a little extra time to explore the meaning of what you are reading and write out your insights in your journal or notebook.

Early in my relationship with God I became confused about what to do with the Bible. I knew I should spend quiet time with God. I knew that reading the Bible was a part of that quiet time.

Then I heard people talk about Bible study. I wondered, *When am I supposed to do that? In my quiet time? Or at another time?* Perhaps you have had these same questions. Over the years I have learned how to incorporate devotional Bible study into my quiet time. The Greek word translated *devote* is *prokarteo* and means to tarry, remain somewhere, or remain long with the thought. In devotional Bible study, we want to tarry awhile in the Word of God in our quiet time. I love Merrill C. Tenney's definition of devotional Bible study:

> Devotional study impresses the message on a believing heart. The crown of all study is devotional study. Devotional study is not so much of a technique as a spirit. It is the spirit of eagerness which seeks the mind of God; it is the spirit of humility which listens readily to the voice of God; it is the spirit of adventure which pursues earnestly the will of God; it is the spirit of adoration which rests in the presence of God.[1]

Early on, I noticed that Amy Carmichael, in her devotional book *The Edges of His Ways*, shared many insights from the Bible: a new observation, a special insight on a verse, application of the verse to an experience, a different translation of a verse, the definition of a word in a verse, or several verses related to a topic. I realized that what she shared was a result of her devotional quiet time in the Word. I thought to myself, *Why can't I incorporate these devotional studies into my quiet time as well?* And so I decided to become creative as I sat with God in His Word. Learning principles of biblical interpretation in seminary has also added new ideas for devotional Bible study in my quiet time.

Devotional Bible study means taking time in your Bible reading to tarry awhile to discover God's secrets and meet Him face-to-face. When you read your passage of Scripture in your quiet time, you will notice a significant word, phrase, person, or verse. Take some time to look for one of the following opportunities to dig deeper when you read and study God's Word:

- *Observation study.* Do you notice a group of interesting facts about a topic such as faith in Hebrews 11, or a person, such as Jesus in John 1? You can make a list of what you notice. You will be amazed at the profound insight that can come from looking more closely at a passage of Scripture and writing out what you see.
- *Translation study.* Is a particular verse meaningful to you in your quiet time? You can look it up in another translation. Sometimes another translation helps you see something new and profound in a verse that you never saw before.
- *Reference or topical study.* Is a certain phrase in a verse or topic significant to you in your quiet time? You can look at other verses in the Bible that relate to your cho-

sen phrase or topic. Looking at other verses helps reveal the meaning of the Word of God.

- *Verse study.* Does a verse contain words you would like to understand better? You can look up the meanings of all those words in exciting word study tools.
- *Word study.* Does your Bible reading include one word that you would like to define? You can look up its meaning in several word study dictionaries.
- *Character study.* Would you like to know more about a biblical character in your Bible reading? You can take time to study people's lives and record insights that will apply to your own life.
- *Doctrine or ethics study.* Would you like to become more clear about what you believe? You can collect verses related to a particular subject.

In devotional Bible study, you read the Bible, write out what you are learning, and allow God's Word to make its way into the deepest places of your heart. Devotional Bible study is not something you will necessarily have time to do every day. You will not use all these techniques at once. But you want to go deeper on some days. These ways to dig deeper will help you do exactly that—go deeper for treasure in the Bible. Devotional study takes only an additional five to ten minutes of your quiet time. Or it can take longer, depending on how much time you have and how much time you are willing to give. Devotional study is not meant to take the place of inductive Bible study in a particular book of the Bible. It is meant to take you deeper in your Bible reading, day by day. It allows you to learn powerful truths from God. Devotional Bible study is what you can do any day of the week during your quiet time. And when you do, you will discover God's magnificent secrets.

Discovering the Secrets

Here are just a few examples of the secrets of God I have discovered in His Word:

- *The secret of contentment.* "In any and every circumstance I have learned the secret of being filled and going hungry, both of having abundance and suffering need" (Philippians 4:12). I remember when I first discovered this verse; it helped me understand that contentment in life depends on my relationship with the Lord and not my outward circumstances.
- *The secret of weakness.* "'Power is perfected in weakness.' Most gladly, therefore, I will rather boast about my weaknesses, so that the power of Christ may dwell in

me...for when I am weak, then I am strong" (2 Corinthians 12:9-10). When I discovered this verse, I learned that God can do great and mighty things in and through me even when I am weak.

- *The secret of the inner life.* "But when you pray, go into your room and shut the door and pray to your Father who is in secret. And your Father who sees in secret will reward you" (Matthew 6:6 ESV). This is a powerful secret because it demonstrates that my quiet time with God is important to Him.
- *The secret of faith.* "We walk by faith, not by sight" (2 Corinthians 5:7 ESV). This verse shows me the secret about how I am to live my life, taking God at His Word by faith.
- *The secret of the kingdom of God.* "To you it has been given to know the secrets of the kingdom of God" (Luke 8:10 ESV). This verse tells me that all of life is wrapped up in God's kingdom, not the things of this world.
- *The secret of the future.* "I will show you secrets you have never known" (Isaiah 48:6 ESV). This secret helps me understand that God knows the future, and He lets His children know what we need to know in advance. A great example is the book of Revelation, where God lets me know "the rest of the story."

God will reveal literally hundreds if not thousands of secrets to you when you draw near to Him in His Word. As Paul told the church at Corinth, "No mere man has ever seen, heard, or even imagined what wonderful things God has ready for those who love the Lord" (1 Corinthians 2:9 TLB).

Chapter 3

DEVOTIONAL BIBLE STUDIES

Angels would have given anything to be in on this.
1 Peter 1:12 MSG

Every day is a new day when you open the pages of your Bible. God wants to show you things you have never seen before. And He often uses your quiet time as the catalyst for surprise. Peter points out that the Holy Spirit reveals truth to us that is so amazing that "even the angels are eagerly watching these things happen" (1 Peter 1:12 NLT). The more you look in the mirror of God's Word, the more you will see. And the more you see, the more you will know your Lord. The more you know Him, the more you will love Him. And the more you love Him, the more you will fall on your knees in worship of Him. The secret is learning new ways to look in the mirror of God's Word.

The following devotional Bible studies are different ways to spend more time with God looking into the mirror of His Word. You will need your Bible and the Devotional Bible Study pages with all the studies in this book. In some studies, additional optional tools are recommended such as a concordance or a word study dictionary.

Examples of each study are also included to help you see how to use these different pages. For additional reading and study about devotional Bible studies and Bible study tools, and for detailed views of different Bible Study tools, please refer to the companion book complementing this notebook, *Knowing and Loving The Bible.*

I want to encourage you to personalize these studies as you read God's Word each day. The best way to learn how to use these pages and incorporate these studies into your quiet time is to actually do it for yourself. If you've never studied the Bible, you might feel as though Bible study is an unattainable goal. I encourage you that the more time you spend in God's Word, the more time you will want to spend in His Word. You will love it more and more as the Holy Spirit brings it alive to you. Read through the instructions for each study, then look at the example to see how these Bible study pages can be used in your quiet time. I've also included some application questions at the end of each set of instructions to help you get started in your studies. You might think of this section as a Bible study workshop for you to grow in devotional Bible study.

Observation Study

Recommended tools: cross-reference Bible

Study goal: to learn spiritual principles for your life related to a biblical word, topic, character, or event

1. Choose a word, topic, character, or event from your passage.
2. Write the subject of your study on the Observation Study page (see example on the next page). Be sure to put today's date so you can keep a chronicle of your journey with the Lord. Then record what passage of Scripture you are studying.
3. As you observe each truth about a repeated word, topic, Bible character, or event, write out what you see, fact by fact. If you have time, record the verses related to each observation.
4. Once you have recorded what you have seen, summarize what you have learned in two to three sentences.
5. Write in one sentence how you can apply what you have learned to your own life.

Suggested observation studies: the Lord in Psalm 139, Ezra in Ezra 7–10, suffering in Philippians, hope in 1 Peter, Jesus in Revelation 1:13-20

Application:

Write out some of your favorite passages of Scripture that you would like to study. Turn to one of them, choose a blank Observation Study page, and make observations about a repeated word, a significant topic, or an outstanding character.

Observation Study

"Be still and know that I am God ... "
— Psalm 46:10 NIV

Scripture Passage Hebrews 11:1-6

Significant Word, Topic, or Character Faith

Observations about a Word, Topic, or Character

Verse & Observations

11:1 - It is the assurance of things hoped for, the conviction of things not seen.
11:2 - It is how men in the past gained God's approval.
11:3 - It is how we understand the invisible things like the creation of the world.
11:4 - It is why Abel's sacrifice was better and it resulted in righteousness.
11:5 - It is why Enoch was pleasing to God and taken without experiencing death
11:6 - Must have it to please God, believes God exists, rewards us if we seek Him

Summary & Conclusions

Faith is concerned with the invisible. It is how we understand the invisible, spiritual world. It is how we gain God's approval. Faith results in righteousness. Faith pleases God.

Application in My Life

I must learn to walk by faith because that is what pleases God. Walking by faith today means that I am going to hope in God.

TRANSLATION STUDY

Recommended tools: NASB, NIV

Optional tools: AMP, NLT, MSG, Williams New Testament, ESV

Study goal: to understand the meaning of a verse by examining various Bible translations with life application

1. Record your verse on a Translation Study page (see example on the next page).
2. Choose at least two translations and write out the verse from each translation word for word. If you have access to the Internet, use the many Bible translations available online at www.biblegateway.com. Without the Internet, use the Comparative Study Bible, which offers four translations (KJV, AMP, NASB, NIV), or Bible study software.
3. Moving from phrase to phrase, examine your verse in each translation and/or paraphrase, and note the differences among the versions. Record your observations.
4. Summarize how your observations provide insight into the meaning of the verse. Choose your favorite translation of the verse and write out why you like it so much.
5. Write in one sentence how you can apply what you have learned to your own life.

Suggested translation studies: Jeremiah 29:11; John 14:26; Romans 12:1-2; Hebrew 1:3, 11:1.

Application:

What translations do you currently have and what translations and/or paraphrases would you like get for your resource library?

What are some of your favorite verses? Choose one and do a translation study.

Selected Verse(s) Hebrews 11:1

Write out, word for word, the selected verse(s) for each translation

Translation & Verses

NASB - Now faith is the assurance of things hoped for, the conviction of things not seen.

NIV - Now faith is being sure of what we hope for, and certain of what we do not see.

AMP - Now faith is the assurance (the confirmation, the title-deed) of the things [we] hope for, being the proof of things [we] do not see and the conviction of their reality (faith perceiving as real fact what is not revealed to the senses).

Observations

Faith is a response to things we hope for and things unseen. It is an assurance, certainty, perceiving as real fact what we cannot see or hear.

Summary & Conclusions

Faith perceives the fact of God's Word, even though my feelings do not always perceive its reality.

Application in My Life

My life can be a demonstration of God's truth when I live by faith.

Verse Study

Recommended tools: exhaustive concordance, *Hebrew-Greek Key Word Study Bible, The Complete Word Study Old Testament* and *New Testament*

Optional tools: *The Complete Word Study Dictionary: New Testament, Theological Wordbook of the Old Testament, Vine's Expository Dictionary, Wuest's Word Studies in the Greek New Testament*

Study goal: to appreciate the beauty of biblical words in their original language, gaining deeper insight into the meaning with life application

1. Select a verse that impresses you, a significant verse from a passage you are reading and studying, and write the complete verse on a Verse Study page (see example on the next page).
2. Choose at least two important words in your verse and write them in the spaces provided on the Verse Study page.
3. Using your exhaustive concordance, Key Word Study Bible, or Complete Word Study Old or New Testament, record the Strong's number for each word in its corresponding space.
4. Using the Key Word Study Bible, The Complete Word Study Old or New Testament, or optional tools, define each word.
5. Review the context of your verse (cultural and biblical context including author and date) through your own observation and by consulting a study Bible, a Bible dictionary or encyclopedia, or a commentary.
6. Review your word definitions and summarize your conclusions on the meaning of your verse.
7. Write in one sentence how you can apply what you have learned to your own life.

Suggested verse studies: Psalm 27:14; Jeremiah 29:11; 31:3; John 1:14; 3:16; Ephesians 1:7,18; 3:17; 6:12; Hebrews 1:3; 11:1; James 1:3;4:8

Application:

What are some of your favorite verses in the Bible or verses that you would like to understand in a deeper way.

Verse–Passage

Hebrews 11:1 Now faith is the assurance of things hoped for, the conviction of things not seen.

Word(s): Faith — Strong's #: 4102
Source: Key Word Study Bible & CWStudy NT — Hebrew–Greek: Pistis
Meaning: Being persuaded, faith, belief. Implies such a knowledge, assent, and confidence that it results in good works.

Word(s): Assurance — Strong's #: 5287
Source: Key Word Study Bible & CWStudy NT — Hebrew–Greek: Hupostasis
Meaning: Firm confidence, constancy, confident expectation.

Word(s): Hoped for — Strong's #: 1679
Source: Key Word Study Bible & CWStudy NT — Hebrew–Greek: Elpizo
Meaning: Hope, expect with desire. To set my hope in something. Hope for a good future.

Word(s): Conviction — Strong's #: 1650
Source: Key Word Study Bible & CWStudy NT — Hebrew–Greek: Elegchos
Meaning: Such a conviction of things not seen that those truths are manifested and results are reaped in my life.

Summary & Conclusions

Faith is more than assent. Faith makes the unseen visible as it produces outward manifestation in my life i.e. good works.

Application in My Life

I desire and need faith. God expects me to have such a confident expectation in His promises that it produces a change in me and results in a glorification of Him in everything I do.

WORD STUDY

Recommended tools: exhaustive concordance, *Hebrew-Greek Key Word Study Bible, The Complete Word Study Old and New Testament,* Hebrew concordance coded to Strong's

Optional tools: *The Complete Word Study Dictionary: New Testament, Theological Wordbook of the Old Testament, Vine's Expository Dictionary, Wuest's Word Studies in the Greek New Testament, Linguistic Key to the Greek New Testament*

Study goal: to gain a more complete picture of the meaning of a word in the original Greek or Hebrew with life application

1. Select a word that impresses you, a significant word from a passage you are reading and studying, and record the word on a Word Study page (see example following these instructions).
2. Using your exhaustive concordance, *Key Word Study Bible*, or *The Complete Word Study Old or New Testament*, record the Strong's number for your word.
3. Record the Scripture passage that contains the word.
4. Record the Hebrew or Greek transliteration of your word (the English phonetic equivalent for the Hebrew or Greek word. You can find this in the lexical aids in the *Key Word Study Bible* or the Strong's dictionary).
5. Record any other ways this Hebrew or Greek word has been translated into English by looking in other English translations of the Bible.
6. Look in the Strong's Exhaustive Concordance dictionary and write out the brief definition in your notebook or on the Word Study page.
7. Look up the word in *Vine's Expository Dictionary* (if available) and record its definition.
8. Record definitions from either the *Key Word Study Bible, The Complete Word Study New or Old Testament* lexical aids, *The Complete Word Study Dictionary: New Testament*, or *Theological Wordbook of the Old Testament* (if available).
9. Choose any additional word study tools (if available) and record the definitions. Make certain that additional word study tools are keyed to the Strong's numbers if you do not know the original Hebrew and Greek languages. Some word study tools

such as *Wuest's Word Studies in the Greek New Testament* are written in verse order for certain books of the Bible. These types of tools are especially easy to use since you only need to look up the chapter and verse and then read all that the author has to say about the words in that verse

10. Using the Greek concordance found in back of *The Complete Word Study New Testament*, or a Hebrew or Greek concordance keyed to the Strong's numbers such as *Wigram's Englishman's Hebrew Concordance* or Greek Concordance, look up your Hebrew or Greek word using the Strong's number. Record all the verses using your word from the book of the Bible containing the word you are studying. As you look up each verse and record your insights, you will be learning how the author has used this same Hebrew or Greek word in other parts of the book God has inspired him to write.
11. Record other verses found in the Old or New Testament that contain your Hebrew or Greek word. As you look up each verse and record your insights, you will be learning how other authors have used this same Hebrew or Greek word.
12. Review all your definitions and summarize what you believe this word means.
13. To keep your word definition in context, write in one sentence why the author chose this word and how it helps you understand the selected verse or passage of study.
14. Write in one sentence how you can apply what you have learned to your own life.

Suggested word studies: *faith* in Hebrews 11:1, *perseverance* in James 1:12, *blessed* in Matthew 5:3, *love* in 1 Corinthians 13:1, *prayed* in James 5:17, *humbled* in Philippians 2:8

Application:

What are some words in the Bible that you would like to study? Choose one of your favorite words in the Bible, and study it using one of the Word Study pages.

What Bible study tools would you like for your resource library to accomplish Word studies?

Word(s): Faith
Strong's #: 4102
Other Translations: Believe, Trust
Hebrew–Greek: Pistis
Scripture Passage for Word(s): Hebrews 11

Strong's Concordance

Faith, faithfulness, pledge, proof

Vine's Expository Dictionary

Believing, trusting, relying

Key Word Study Bible, Complete Word Study NT&OT, Theological WB OT, Dictionaries

Used 6 ways 1. being persuaded, knowledge of, assent to, confidence in God's truth resulting in good works. 2. resulting in miracles during Christ's time on earth. 3. promising justification and salvation 4. Christian religion. 5. Fidelity 6. Assurance, proof. in Complete Word Study New Testament

Linguistic Key To The Greek NT, Wuest's Word Studies, Brown's Dictionary of NT Theology, Robertson's Word Pictures, Commentaries

Linguistic Key p. 706: to understand. A mental perception.

Wuest Vol 2, p. 193: Faith apprehends as real fact what is not revealed to the senses. It rests on that fact, acts upon it, and is upheld by it in the face of all that seems to contradict it. Faith is real sight.

Brown, Vol 1, p. 593-605: Man's trust presents the possibility for God to do His work. Not wild enthusiasm. Wrestle with God. Directed towards reality, deeply involved in the act of living.

Other Uses in Immediate Area of Study

Used 32 times in Hebrews. 4:2 Word (logos) doesn't profit if not united with faith. 6:11 a believer's foundation. 6:12 necessary to inherit promises - results in patience. 10:22 how we are to draw near. 10:38 how we are to live 10:39 preserves the soul. 12:2 Jesus is the author and finisher of our faith. 13:7 we are to imitate the faith of our leaders.

Other Uses in Old & New Testament

Matt 8:10 centurion is example of great faith. Acts 3:16 our faith is from Jesus and is to be in His name. Rom 1:5 involves obedience 1:12 our faith can encourage others. 1:17 how the righteous are to live 4:9 Abraham an example of faith. 5:1-2 how we are introduced into the grace of God. 12:3 each is alloted a measure of faith. 12:6 we are to exercise our gifts according to our proportion of faith. 14:23 if not from faith then is sin. James 1:3 testing of faith produces endurance. 2:17 true faith accompanied by works. 1 Pet 1:7 Genuine faith more precious than gold.

Summary & Conclusions

1. Faith is how we live and is essential to experiencing all that God promises. 2. Our faith is in God's Word. 3. Faith results in patience, righteousness, justification, salvation, endurance, and the experience of God's grace. 4. I am given a measure of faith and am to exercise gifts accordingly. 5. As a leader, I must demonstrate faith.

Meaning in Present Study

Hebrews 11 is the hall of fame of faith. Contains numerous examples of those who held strong to promises of God with good works and glorified God.

Application in My Life

I am challenged to have a life characterized by biblical faith. This means I am to be obedient to God, patient, and endure all trials and temptations. I can never give up. I must believe God for all things I believe He has called me to do.

REFERENCE STUDY

Recommended tools: cross-reference Bible

Optional tools: *The New Treasury of Scripture Knowledge*

Study goal: to discover the whole counsel of God's Word about the meaning of a particular phrase in the Bible with life application

1. Select a favorite phrase from the Bible.
2. Find the letter of the alphabet at the beginning of the selected phrase in your cross-reference Bible.
3. Find the verse number in the margin and the letter of the alphabet following that number. Next to the letter will be one or more cross-references.
4. Write down each reference on a Reference Study page (see example on the next page).
5. Look up each reference in your Bible and write out your insights.
6. Summarize what you have learned from your study.
7. Write in one sentence how you can apply what you have learned to your own life.

Suggested reference studies: Psalm 46:1; 84:11; 91:1; John 1:1; 16:33; Ephesians 1:3; Philippians 4:6-7

Application:

What are some of your favorite verses in the Bible? List them here, then do a reference study with each one.

REFERENCE STUDY

PAGE ONE

"…the grass withers and the flowers fall but the word of the Lord stands forever." — 1 Peter 1:24-25 NIV

Verse–Topic Faith *Scripture* Hebrews 11:1

Record observations and insights from the following references related to the selected verse or topic. Define any key words.

Key Words–Definitions

Faith—confidence in divine truth (Taken from Key Word Study Bible)

2 Samuel 22:31

Reference

God's way is perfect—He is a refuge (buckler KJV) for those who trust Him.

Psalm 51:1

Reference

When I trust (put my faith in) God, I can rejoice—He will defend me.

Psalm 9:10

Reference

Knowing God's name (His ways and character) will help me trust.

Romans 1:17

Reference

I am to live by faith.

Romans 5:1

Reference

I am justified by faith and, as a result, I am given peace through Christ.

Romans 10:17

Reference

Faith comes from hearing, and hearing from the Word of Christ.

1 Corinthians 2:5

Reference

My faith does not rest in the wisdom of men, but the power of God.

Ephesians 6:16

Reference

Faith is my shield in spiritual warfare.

Summary–Conclusions

1. Trust in God demonstrates my faith.
2. I am to live by faith.
3. Faith comes from hearing the word of Christ.
4. If I want to have faith, I must be in the Word, and come to know God and His ways.
5. Faith is a powerful weapon in spiritual warfare.

Application in My Life

Lord, today I see how important my demonstration of faith and trust in You is. I see the importance of knowing You in Your Word. Help me to make Your Word a priority.

Topical Study

Recommended tools: cross-reference Bible, concordance

Optional tools: *Nave's Topical Bible*

Study goal: to discover the whole counsel of God's Word about a topic in the Bible with life application. This is another type of reference study and uses the same style of page.

1. Select a favorite word or topic from the Bible.
2. Look in *Nave's Topical Bible* or a concordance and find that word.
3. Write down as many of the references as desired on a Topical Study page (see example on the next page).
4. Look up each verse in your Bible and write out your insights.
5. Summarize what you have learned from your study.
6. Write in one sentence how you can apply what you have learned to your own life.

Suggested topical studies: hope, trust, joy, Jesus, love, peace, marriage, children, suffering, holiness

Application:

What are some of your favorite words and topics in the Bible? Write them out below as you read through God's Word. Then, as God leads you, do a topical study using the pages in this notebook.

TOPICAL STUDY

PAGE ONE

"…the grass withers and the flowers fall but the word of the Lord stands forever." — 1 Peter 1:24-25 NIV

Verse–Topic Hope *Scripture* Hebrews 11:1

Record observations and insights from the following references related to the selected verse or topic. Define any key words.

Key Words–Definitions

Hope—elpizo from elpis (1679, 1680 Strong's), expect with desire, desire of some good with expectation of obtaining it. (Taken from Key Word Study Bible)

Psalm 39:7

Reference

My hope is in the Lord

Romans 5:5

Reference

Hope never disappoints because God's love is poured out within my heart through the Holy Spirit

Romans 15:4

Reference

I am given hope through perseverance and the encouragement of the Scriptures

Romans 15:13

Reference

God is a God of hope. When I believe God, He fills me with all joy and peace, so I will abound in hope by the power of the Holy Spirit.

Titus 3:7

Reference

Eternal life gives me hope because I am justified by God's grace and made an heir

Hebrews 11:1

Reference

Faith is the evidence of the things I hope for

1 Peter 1:3

Reference

I am born again to a living hope through the resurrection of Christ

1 Peter 3:15

Reference

I should always be ready to give an account for the hope that is in me.

Summary–Conclusions

1. God is the source of my hope and the object of my hope.
2. My hope is a sure thing and will never let me down.
3. Hope comes from the Word of God.
4. God wants me to overflow with hope so that I always have more than enough.
5. My faith is closely related to hope, and shows how much hope I have.
6. God wants me to share my hope with others when given the opportunity.

Application in My Life

Lord, today I am so thankful for the gift of hope. Help me to turn to You, open Your Word, believe what You say, and overflow with hope. Thank you for being the God of hope and giving me more than enough hope. In Jesus' name, Amen.

CHARACTER STUDY

Recommended tools: cross-reference Bible, exhaustive concordance

Optional tools: Nave's Topical Bible, Thompson Chain Reference Bible, International Standard Bible Encyclopedia, New Bible Dictionary

Study goal: Your goal in this study is to form spiritual principles from a Bible character's life that will help you walk more closely with the Lord. Sometimes your key passages will be your immediate area of study. Other times your immediate area of study simply mentions the person's name, and you need to search out the main passages using a concordance, topical Bible, or Bible dictionary or encyclopedia. This can be accomplished by cross-referencing the verse in the immediate area of study, by looking up the person's name in your exhaustive concordance, and by looking up the person's name in *Nave's Topical Bible* or in the back of *Thompson Chain Reference Bible.*

1. Record the character you have chosen and the area of study that prompted you to choose this person on a Character Study page (see example on the next page).
2. Once you find the person's name, write down the most frequently referenced passages in your journal or on a Character Study page.
3. You may choose to look at each passage, recording your observations. However, it is most beneficial to choose only one or two main passages to study in one sitting. This allows you to spend more time making observations. Turn to a number of the passages, asking God to guide you in your choice of passages.
4. Read your chosen passages slowly, verse by verse, recording as you read

- What you notice about this person's life.
- Insights related to their character.
- The important events in their life.
- The quality of their relationship with God.

5. Write your observations.
6. After you have read verse by verse, recording your observations, think about what you have observed. Summarize your significant observations of their life, major character qualities, important life events, and relationship with God. Write a summary.

7. Using the *International Standard Bible Encyclopedia,* the *New Bible Dictionary,* or other encyclopedias, dictionaries, and biographies, record any additional insights.
8. Summarize significant principles learned from the person's life.
9. Write in one sentence how you can apply what you have learned to your own life.

Suggested Character Studies: Abraham in Genesis 12–15; 22; *Joseph* in Genesis 37–45; *Moses* in Exodus 3; *Joshua* in Joshua 1–8; 23–24; *Deborah* in Judges 4–5; *Ruth* in Ruth 1–4; *David* in 1 Samuel 16–17; *David* in 2 Samuel 5–9; 11–12; 22–24; *Mary* in Luke 1–2; *Elizabeth* and *Zacharias* in Luke 1; *Saul/Paul* in Acts 7:57–9:31; and *John* in Revelation 1; 22.

Application:

What are some of your favorite characters in the Bible? Choose from your favorites and/or from one of the suggested character studies and spend time studying God's Word using the Character Study pages in this notebook.

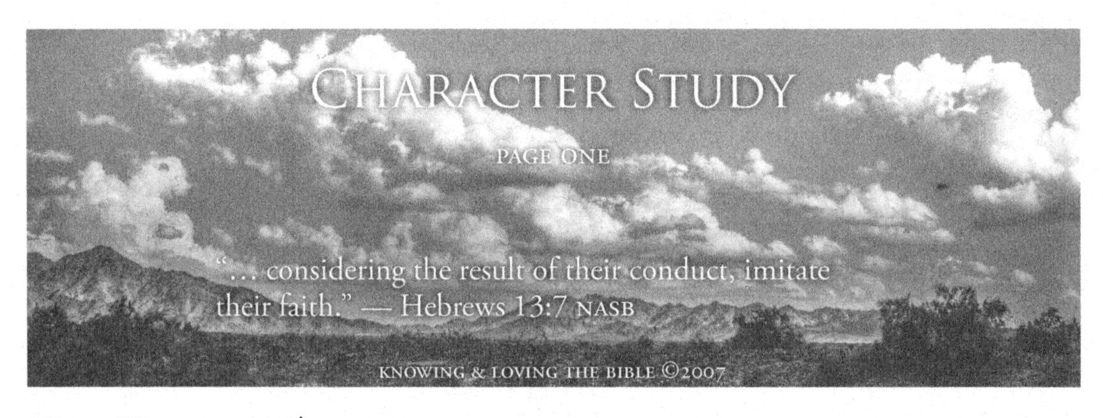

Verse–Topic Noah

Area of Study Hebrews 11

Key Scripture Passages Genesis 6-9

Record observations of life, insights of character, important events, relationship with God

Verse & Observations

6:8 - In midst of wickedness on earth, Noah found favor with God.

6:9 - Noah a righteous man, blameless in his time Noah walked with God.

6:10 - A father of 3 sons

6:14 - Commanded to build an ark

6:22 - Noah did everything the Lord commanded him to do

7:1 - Noah was the only one God considered righteous in his time

7:1-24 - Major Event: Noah and his family survived the flood, protected in ark, lone survivors.

8:1 - God remembered Noah

8:10, 12 - Possessed the ability to wait

8:20 - First thing he did after leaving ark: built an altar to the Lord, an aroma soothing to the Lord

9:1 - God blessed Noah and his sons, caused them to be fruitful

9:11 - God established a covenant with Noah

9:20-24 - Noah became drunk with wine - devastating results

9:29 - Noah lived 950 years, then died

Significant Observations of Character's Life

Noah was a father. Had 3 sons. Was able to build an ark. Lived 950 years.

Major Character Qualities

A righteous man. Blameless in his time. Walked with God. Did all God commanded him to do. He was obedient.

Important Life Events

Lived in a corrupt world. Experienced the flood.

Relationship with God

Had an intimate relationship with God. He walked with God. Was not afraid to stand blameless, alone in the midst of a corrupt world.

Information from other Sources

New Bible Dictionary, p. 837-838 He was the last of 10 patriarchs. Son of Lamech. Name associated with verb meaning comfort and relief. His life: possessed righteousness that comes from faith. Close communion with God. Covenant with Noah - God promised to never again destroy mankind with a flood.

Significant Principles Summary

1. It is possible to walk with God in the idst of a corrupt and evil world even if I am the only one.

2. It pays to have a life of obedience to God's commands, to be righteous,and to walk with God.

Application in My Life

Corruption around me is no excuse for sin. God expects me to live by faith, with His commands as my standard.

DOCTRINE OR ETHICS STUDY

Recommended tools: cross-reference Bible, Quiet Time Notebook, exhaustive concordance

Optional tools: Nave's Topical Bible, Thompson Chain Reference Bible, The Moody Handbook of Theology, Encyclopedia of Biblical and Christian Ethics, International Standard Bible Encyclopedia, New Bible Dictionary

Study goal: to know what you believe and apply it to your life

1. Select a doctrine or ethic and write the topic in your journal or on a Doctrine or Ethics page (see example on the next page).
2. Record relevant Scriptures you have found in your daily Bible reading, your exhaustive concordance, *Nave's Topical Bible,* or *Thompson Chain Reference Bible.*
3. Next to each verse, write in one sentence how it sheds light on your selected doctrine or ethic.
4. Define any important words that are relevant to the doctrine or ethic.
5. Search other reference works, such as *The Moody Handbook of Theology, Encyclopedia of Biblical and Christian Ethics, International Standard Bible Encyclopedia,* and the *New Bible Dictionary* to learn more about your doctrine or ethic and to find any additional related verses.
6. Summarize your beliefs based on your findings.
7. Write in one sentence how you can apply what you have learned to your own life.

Suggested doctrine studies: the attributes and names of God, the attributes and names of Jesus Christ, the humanity and divinity of Christ, the Holy Spirit, the Trinity, man, sin, salvation, eternal security, the church, angels, future things (judgment, heaven, hell, the return of Christ, death, eternity). For additional specific doctrines, consult *The Moody Handbook of Theology.*

Suggested ethic studies: abortion, affluence, alcohol and social drinking, cheating, church and state, employment and work, family, fidelity and morality, homosexuality, leisure, lying and truthfulness, marriage, war, women in ministry, observing the Sabbath. For additional specific ethical issues consult *Encyclopedia of Biblical and Christian Ethics.*

Application:

Choose one of the suggested doctrine/ethics studies and study God's Word to learn more.

DOCTRINE-ETHICS STUDY

PAGE ONE

"If you are asked about your Christian hope, always be ready to explain it." — 1 Peter 3:15 TLB

Doctrine–Ethic The Holy Spirit

Record Scripture references related to selected doctrine/ethic & include insights gained from your study.

John 3:5
Reference

Must be born of the Spirit to enter the kingdom of God

John 14:16
Reference

The Holy Spirit is a Comforter given to us by the Father. Abides with us forever. Will be in us. Teaches us all things. Brings Jesus' words to our remembrance. Convicts the world.

Acts 1:5-8
Reference

We are to be baptized in the Holy Spirit. Gives us the power to be God's witnesses.

Romans 5:5
Reference

The Holy Spirit sheds the love of God abroad in our hearts.

Romans 8
Reference

Sets me free from the law of sin and death. Dwells in me. Must have to belong to God. Makes intercession for us according to will of God.

Doctrine–Ethic The Holy Spirit

Galatians 5:22
Reference

Fruit of the Spirit is love, joy, peace, patience, kindness, goodness, faithfulness, gentleness, self-control.

Ephesians 5:18
Reference

We are to be filled with the Holy Spirit.

1 Thessalonians 5:19
Reference

We are not to quench the Holy Spirit.

Additional Related Scripture References:

Genesis 1:2, Luke 2:12, Acts 10, 2 Corinthians 10:18, 2 Thessalonians 2:13, 1 John 5:6 2 Corinthians 1:22 (seals us), changes and sanctifies us.

Word Definitions

filled (4137): control. quench (4570): to put out (a fire). Spirit: pneuma

Commentaries

Moody (p. 245-281: HS has intellect, knowledge, mind, emotions, will. 1 Cor. 2:11 is deity. Divine works: creation, inspiration of Scripture, regeneration, intercession, sanctification.

Summarize Beliefs Related to Selected Doctrine-Ethic

Holy Spirit is 3rd Person of the Triune God. I am indwelt by the HS at time of salvation, filled/controlled by HS continuously. He changes me and produces fruit in my life consistent with kingdom of God. Intercedes for me. I am never to put out (quench) the HS.

Chapter 4

HOW TO USE THE DEVOTIONAL BIBLE STUDY NOTEBOOK

Be diligent to present yourself approved to God as a workman who does not need to be ashamed, accurately handling the word of truth
2 Timothy 2:15

Spending time alone with God in His Word will transform everything in your life. God speaks in His Word through the power of the Holy Spirit. When you draw near to Him and listen to Him speak, you will never be the same. You will become more and more like Christ as you respond to what God says in wholehearted devotion and surrender. You will be revived, renewed and transformed. You will build your life on a firm foundation that cannot be shaken when trials come your way. You will come to know God more as you discover who He is, what He does, and what He says. You will pray more and experience His peace. And you will walk with hope as you grasp the magnificent promises of God found on every page in the Bible. All of this and more awaits you as you spend time studying God's Word.

The Devotional Bible Study Notebook, with eight different studies and corresponding pages, will help you dig deeper in God's Word. So, where do you begin? The best way is to do one of each of the eight studies, using the pages you will find in the next section of this notebook. You might begin with an Observation study. Choose a favorite passage of Scripture, pray and ask the Lord to speak to you, then read the passage, writing out everything you see in the verses. At first, you may wonder if you are "doing it right." I felt the same way when I first began living in God's Word. Let me just release you from that idea and encourage you to experiment with these studies. Ask the Lord to teach you and guide you as you draw near to Him in His Word. You will begin to sense that He is the One leading you on this great adventure. After all, the Word of God is a gift from Him. He has given the Bible to you with great purpose, so He wants you to know what He has to say even more than you desire it right now. With time and practice, these studies will become almost second nature to you. You will have favorites that you will enjoy the most.

So how do these studies work with your quiet time? Every day you will want to read the Bible using a Bible reading plan such as your current Bible study, a Bible reading guide such as

Encounter With God by Scripture Union, or simply reading one chapter a day in a book of the Bible like John or the Psalms. As you read, ask God to speak to you. Look for something significant—it may be a word, phrase, verse, or person in the passage of Scripture. Then, depending on how much time you have, look at these studies and choose one that seems relevant. Perhaps you want to write simple thoughts and observations. Choose the Observation Study. Maybe a verse is significant. You can take that one verse and do a Translation study or a Verse study. Perhaps a phrase is significant to you. You can do a Reference Study. Maybe a word stands out to you, like "hope" or "endurance." You can do a Word study or even a Topical study. Maybe you will be impressed with a person like David or Paul, and you decide to take some time and do a Character study. Or you may be moved by the whole subject of salvation and decide to take time to study the doctrine of salvation—i.e. how we are saved and what Jesus did that accomplishes salvation for us.

And so now, the adventure really begins. As you begin your adventure in God's Word, I invite you to take time alone with the Lord in the quiet time that follows, "Exploring The Romance." And then, know that Bible study is an adventure of learning and growing throughout your life. Studying God's Word is an experience that grows deeper and more precious with time. Some of the greatest treasure is not on the surface, but discovered as you live in a passage of Scripture. So, dear friend, whether you are a seasoned traveler with the Lord or have just begun the journey, I want to pray for your time with Him in His Word.

My Prayer For You

Lord Jesus, I pray for this one who has Your Word and desires to know You more. They have The Devotional Bible Study Notebook and are ready to embark on a new adventure in Your Word. I ask that You will ignite in their heart a deeper passion for You, and speak to them as they read Your Word. Please guide them through the power of the Holy Spirit, giving them magnificent insights. Open their eyes that they may behold wondrous truth in Your Word. And transform their hearts, making them the person You want them to be. May they glorify You, and may they walk wholeheartedly with You every day of their life on earth. And may they someday hear those wonderful words from You when they see You face to face: "Well done, good and faithful servant." In Jesus' Name, Amen. — Catherine Martin

Chapter 5

EXPLORING THE ROMANCE

This book of the law shall not depart from your mouth, but you shall meditate on it day and night.
Joshua 1:8

Prepare Your Heart

G. Campbell Morgan, one of the greatest preachers of the nineteenth century, experienced a crisis of faith when he was a young man. He was so desperate that he locked every book he owned in a cupboard, bought a new Bible, and began to read it. He said, "If it be the Word of God, and if I come to it with an unprejudiced and open mind, it will bring assurance to my soul of itself." He canceled every speaking engagement and devoted all his time to studying the Bible. What was the result? He exclaimed, "The Bible found me!" G. Campbell Morgan went on to become one of the great students of the Word of God. He said, "Of all literature none demands more diligent application than that of the Divine Library." His study began at 6:00 am and lasted without interruption until noon. He read a book of the Bible 40 or 50 times before writing or preaching on it.

G. Campbell Morgan truly discovered the great romance of God and His Word. Everything else paled in comparison to the magnificence of the Bible. Have you made that discovery? As you begin your quiet time, meditate on Psalm 19. Record your most significant insights about the Word of God. Then ask God to speak to your heart today.

Read and Study God's Word

1. Throughout the Bible, God encourages His people to give time and effort to be in His Word. Joshua faced a daunting task—he was Moses' successor to lead the people of Israel into the promised land. Read Joshua 1:1-9 and write all that you learn about the Law (God's Word) and what God wanted Joshua to do with the Law.

2. Look at the following verses and record what you learn about what to do with God's Word:

Colossians 3:16

2 Timothy 2:15

2 Timothy 3:16-17

3. Summarize in two or three sentences what you have learned about the Word of God today.

Adore God in Prayer

Pray the words of this prayer by Amy Carmichael:

Let me see Thy face, Lord Jesus

Caring not for aught beside;

Let me hear Thy voice, Lord Jesus,

Till my soul is satisfied.

Let me walk with Thee, Lord Jesus;

Let me walk in step with Thee.

Let me talk with Thee, Lord Jesus;

Let Thy words be clear to me.

Heavenly music, strength and sweetness,

Joy of joys art Thou to me;

O Beloved, my Lord Jesus,

Let me be a joy to Thee.[1]

Yield Yourself to God

Whenever a new vision is presented to the trusting soul a new crisis is created for that soul, and the soul will either obey and march into larger life, or disobey and turn backward. The man or woman who has the largest, fullest knowledge of Christ is the man or woman who is most conscious that he or she has hardly yet begun to see His glory. The Spirit of God, line upon line, precept upon precept, here a little and there a little, with infinite patience, is forevermore unveiling to the eyes of faithful, watching souls the glory of Christ; and as each new glory is revealed it calls the soul to some new adventure, to some new sacrifice; and wherever there is response to the revelation, realization follows. So by this process of illumination and instruction, we grow up in all things into Him Who is the Head, even Christ Jesus. Every response to light means fuller understanding and enlarged capacity for further revelation. The true Christian life is a growth…There is no exhausting of the light and glory and beauty of Christ…Sanctification is progressive, the Spirit of God patiently leading us from point to point in the life of faith and light and love, and forevermore astonishing us with new unveilings of the glory of our Master. For God, who said, "Light shall shine out of darkness," is the One who has shone in our hearts to give the light of the knowledge of the glory of God in the face of Christ (2 Corinthians 4:6).[2]

G. Campbell Morgan

ENJOY HIS PRESENCE

Do you have a passion to engage and explore this great romance of God and His Word? Will you be a G. Campbell Morgan who spends much time with God in His Word and who enjoys intimate, sweet fellowship with Him? Close your time with the Lord today by writing a prayer expressing all that is on your heart.

REST IN HIS LOVE

"Let the word of Christ richly dwell within you, with all wisdom teaching and admonishing one another with psalms and hymns and spiritual songs, singing with thankfulness in your hearts to God" (Colossians 3:16).

THE DEVOTIONAL BIBLE STUDY NOTEBOOK PAGES

Observation Study

"Be still and know that I am God … "
— Psalm 46:10 NIV

Scripture Passage ____________________

Significant Word, Topic, or Character ____________________

Observations about a Word, Topic, or Character

Verse & Observations

Summary & Conclusions

Application in My Life

Scripture Passage ______________________________

Significant Word, Topic, or Character ______________________________

Observations about a Word, Topic, or Character

Verse & Observations

Summary & Conclusions

Application in My Life

OBSERVATION STUDY

"Be still and know that I am God ... "
— Psalm 46:10 NIV

Scripture Passage ______________________________

Significant Word, Topic, or Character ______________________________

Observations about a Word, Topic, or Character

Verse & Observations

Summary & Conclusions

Application in My Life

OBSERVATION STUDY

"Be still and know that I am God ... "
— Psalm 46:10 NIV

Scripture Passage ______________________________

Significant Word, Topic, or Character ______________________________

Observations about a Word, Topic, or Character

Verse & Observations

Summary & Conclusions

Application in My Life

OBSERVATION STUDY

"Be still and know that I am God ... "
— Psalm 46:10 NIV

KNOWING & LOVING THE BIBLE ©2007

Scripture Passage ______________________________

Significant Word, Topic, or Character ______________________________

Observations about a Word, Topic, or Character

Verse & Observations

Summary & Conclusions

Application in My Life

Observation Study

"Be still and know that I am God ... "
— Psalm 46:10 NIV

KNOWING & LOVING THE BIBLE ©2007

Scripture Passage ______________________________

Significant Word, Topic, or Character ______________________________

Observations about a Word, Topic, or Character

Verse & Observations

Summary & Conclusions

Application in My Life

Observation Study

"Be still and know that I am God . . . "
— Psalm 46:10 NIV

Scripture Passage ______________________

Significant Word, Topic, or Character ______________________

Observations about a Word, Topic, or Character

Verse & Observations

Summary & Conclusions

Application in My Life

Scripture Passage ____________________

Significant Word, Topic, or Character ____________________

Observations about a Word, Topic, or Character

Verse & Observations

Summary & Conclusions

Application in My Life

Scripture Passage ______________________________

Significant Word, Topic, or Character ______________________________

Observations about a Word, Topic, or Character

Verse & Observations

Summary & Conclusions

Application in My Life

Scripture Passage ____________________

Significant Word, Topic, or Character ____________________

Observations about a Word, Topic, or Character

Verse & Observations

Summary & Conclusions

Application in My Life

Scripture Passage ______________________________

Significant Word, Topic, or Character ______________________________

Observations about a Word, Topic, or Character

Verse & Observations

Summary & Conclusions

Application in My Life

Scripture Passage ______________________________

Significant Word, Topic, or Character ______________________________

Observations about a Word, Topic, or Character

Verse & Observations

Summary & Conclusions

Application in My Life

Observation Study

"Be still and know that I am God ... "
— Psalm 46:10 NIV

KNOWING & LOVING THE BIBLE ©2007

Scripture Passage ______________________________

Significant Word, Topic, or Character ______________________________

Observations about a Word, Topic, or Character

Verse & Observations

Summary & Conclusions

Application in My Life

Observation Study

"Be still and know that I am God ... "
— Psalm 46:10 NIV

Scripture Passage ______________________________

Significant Word, Topic, or Character ______________________________

Observations about a Word, Topic, or Character

Verse & Observations

Summary & Conclusions

Application in My Life

Observation Study

"Be still and know that I am God . . . "
— Psalm 46:10 NIV

Scripture Passage ______________________________

Significant Word, Topic, or Character ______________________________

Observations about a Word, Topic, or Character

Verse & Observations

Summary & Conclusions

Application in My Life

OBSERVATION STUDY

"Be still and know that I am God ..."
— Psalm 46:10 NIV

Scripture Passage ______________________________

Significant Word, Topic, or Character ______________________________

Observations about a Word, Topic, or Character

Verse & Observations

Summary & Conclusions

Application in My Life

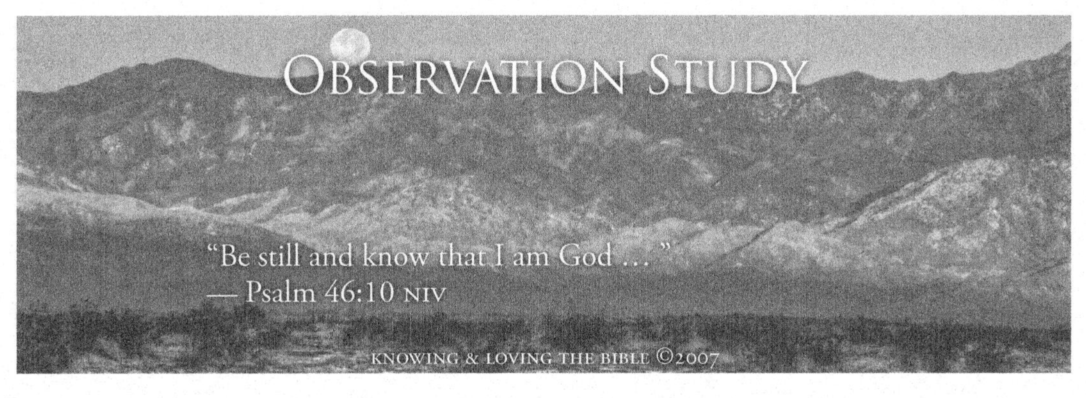

Scripture Passage ______________________________

Significant Word, Topic, or Character ______________________________

Observations about a Word, Topic, or Character

Verse & Observations

Summary & Conclusions

Application in My Life

Scripture Passage ______________________________

Significant Word, Topic, or Character ______________________________

Observations about a Word, Topic, or Character

Verse & Observations

Summary & Conclusions

Application in My Life

Observation Study

"Be still and know that I am God ... "
— Psalm 46:10 NIV

Scripture Passage ____________________

Significant Word, Topic, or Character ____________________

Observations about a Word, Topic, or Character

Verse & Observations

Summary & Conclusions

Application in My Life

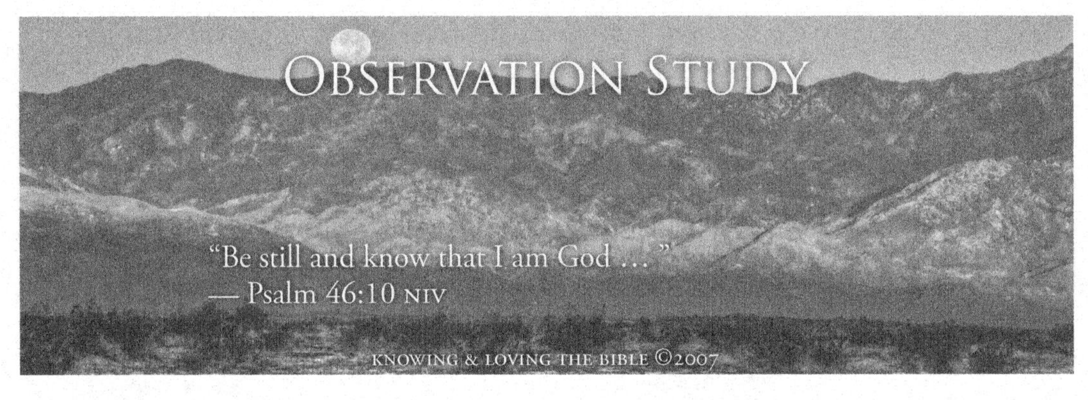

Scripture Passage ______________________________

Significant Word, Topic, or Character ______________________________

Observations about a Word, Topic, or Character

Verse & Observations

Summary & Conclusions

Application in My Life

OBSERVATION STUDY

"Be still and know that I am God ... "
— Psalm 46:10 NIV

Scripture Passage ______________________________

Significant Word, Topic, or Character ______________________________

Observations about a Word, Topic, or Character

Verse & Observations

Summary & Conclusions

Application in My Life

Observation Study

"Be still and know that I am God ... "
— Psalm 46:10 NIV

Scripture Passage ______________________________

Significant Word, Topic, or Character ______________________________

Observations about a Word, Topic, or Character

Verse & Observations

Summary & Conclusions

Application in My Life

Scripture Passage ______________________________

Significant Word, Topic, or Character ______________________________

Observations about a Word, Topic, or Character

Verse & Observations

Summary & Conclusions

Application in My Life

Observation Study

"Be still and know that I am God ... "
— Psalm 46:10 NIV

Scripture Passage ______________________________

Significant Word, Topic, or Character ______________________________

Observations about a Word, Topic, or Character

Verse & Observations

Summary & Conclusions

Application in My Life

Observation Study

"Be still and know that I am God ... "
— Psalm 46:10 NIV

Scripture Passage ______________________________

Significant Word, Topic, or Character ______________________________

Observations about a Word, Topic, or Character

Verse & Observations

Summary & Conclusions

Application in My Life

Scripture Passage ____________________

Significant Word, Topic, or Character ____________________

Observations about a Word, Topic, or Character

Verse & Observations

Summary & Conclusions

Application in My Life

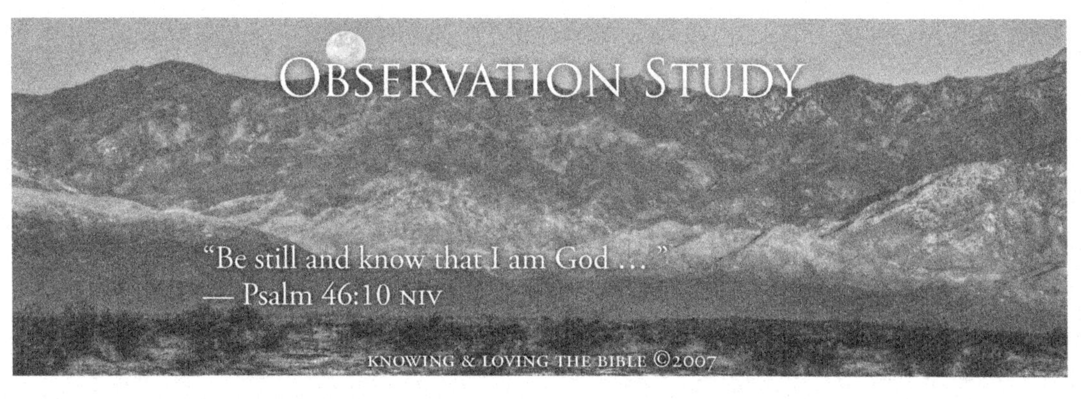

Scripture Passage ______________________________

Significant Word, Topic, or Character ______________________________

Observations about a Word, Topic, or Character

Verse & Observations

Summary & Conclusions

Application in My Life

Observation Study

"Be still and know that I am God ... "
— Psalm 46:10 NIV

Scripture Passage ______________________________

Significant Word, Topic, or Character ______________________________

Observations about a Word, Topic, or Character

Verse & Observations

Summary & Conclusions

Application in My Life

Observation Study

"Be still and know that I am God ... "
— Psalm 46:10 NIV

Scripture Passage ____________________

Significant Word, Topic, or Character ____________________

Observations about a Word, Topic, or Character

Verse & Observations

Summary & Conclusions

Application in My Life

Observation Study

"Be still and know that I am God … "
— Psalm 46:10 NIV

Scripture Passage ______________________________

Significant Word, Topic, or Character ______________________________

Observations about a Word, Topic, or Character

Verse & Observations

Summary & Conclusions

Application in My Life

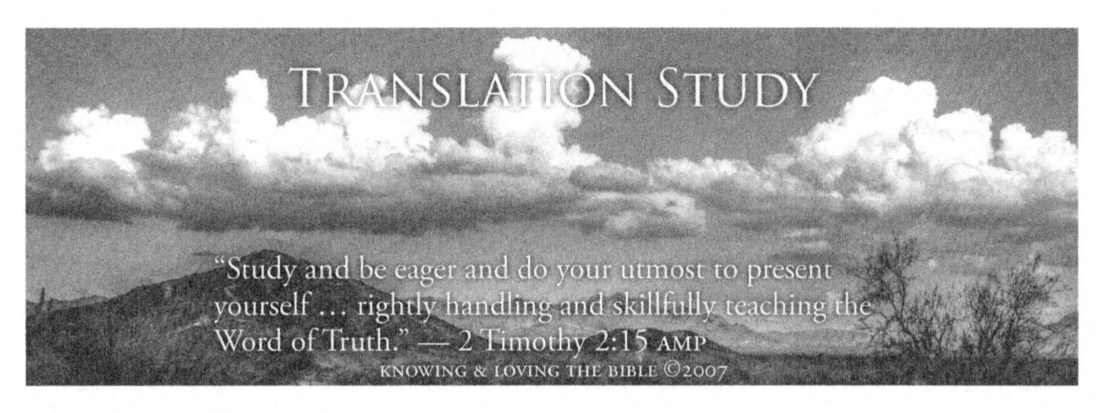

Selected Verse(s) ______________________________

Write out, word for word, the selected verse(s) for each translation

Translation & Verses

Observations

Summary & Conclusions

Application in My Life

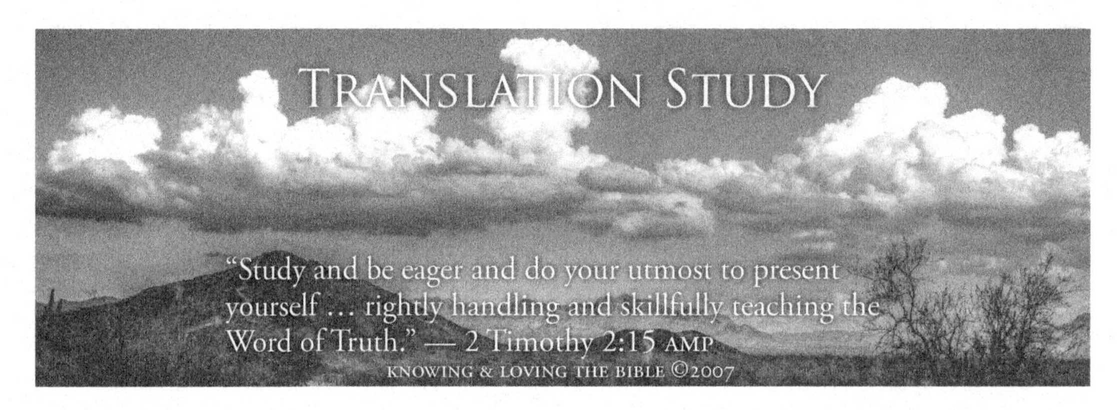

Selected Verse(s) ______________________________

Write out, word for word, the selected verse(s) for each translation

Translation & Verses

Observations

Summary & Conclusions

Application in My Life

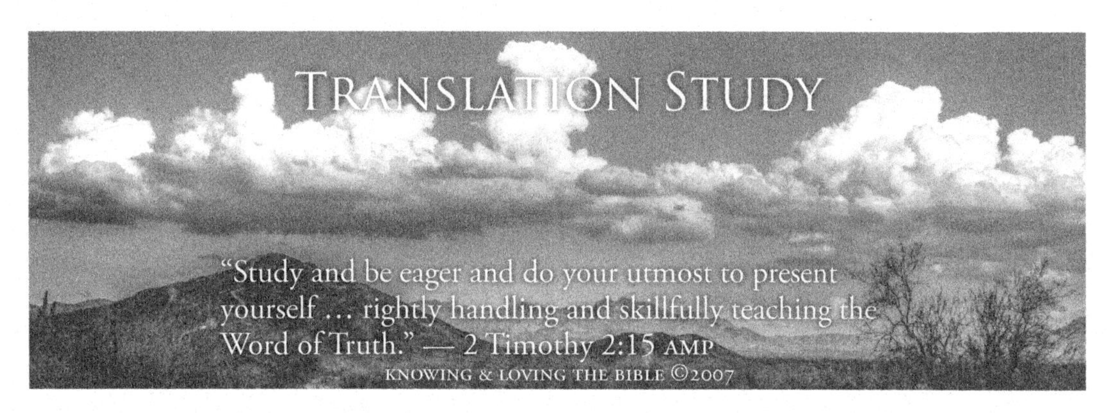

Selected Verse(s) ______________________________

Write out, word for word, the selected verse(s) for each translation

Translation & Verses

Observations

Summary & Conclusions

Application in My Life

Selected Verse(s) ______________________

Write out, word for word, the selected verse(s) for each translation

Translation & Verses

Observations

Summary & Conclusions

Application in My Life

Selected Verse(s) ______________________________

Write out, word for word, the selected verse(s) for each translation

Translation & Verses

Observations

Summary & Conclusions

Application in My Life

Selected Verse(s) ____

Write out, word for word, the selected verse(s) for each translation

Translation & Verses

Observations

Summary & Conclusions

Application in My Life

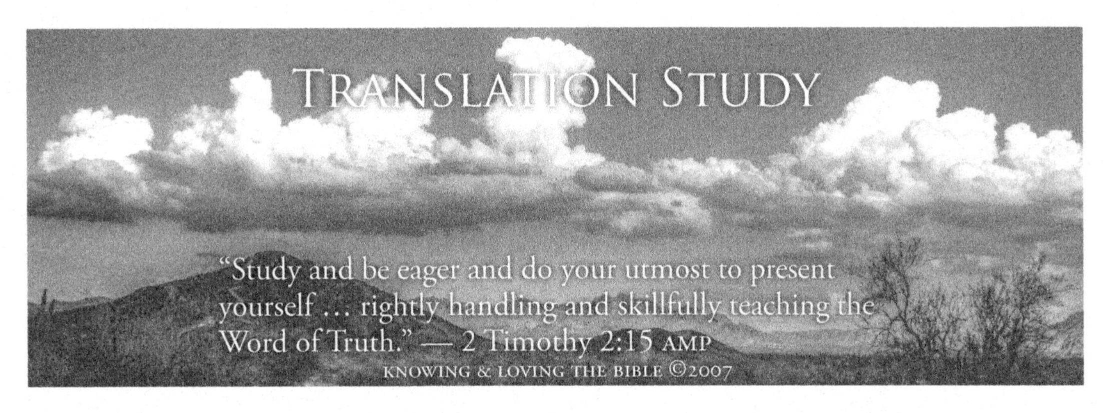

Selected Verse(s) ______________________________

Write out, word for word, the selected verse(s) for each translation

Translation & Verses

Observations

Summary & Conclusions

Application in My Life

Selected Verse(s) ______________________________

Write out, word for word, the selected verse(s) for each translation

Translation & Verses

Observations

Summary & Conclusions

Application in My Life

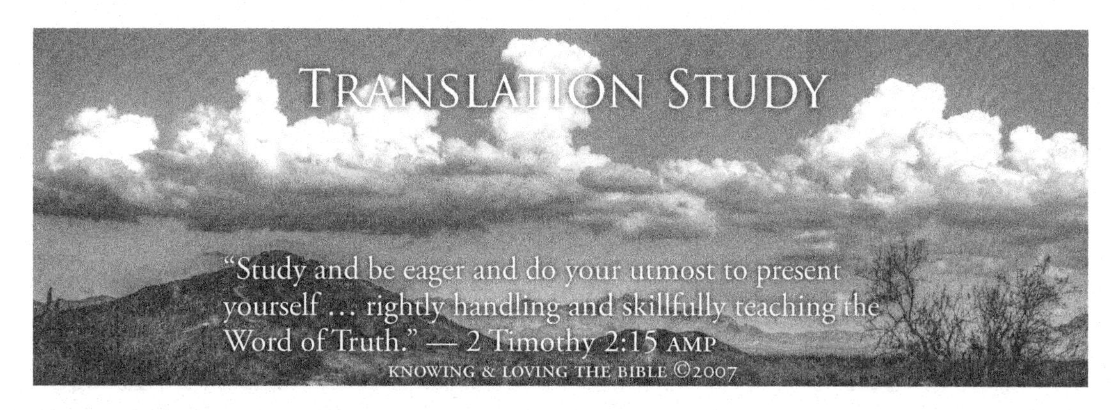

Selected Verse(s) ______________________________

Write out, word for word, the selected verse(s) for each translation

Translation & Verses

Observations

Summary & Conclusions

Application in My Life

Selected Verse(s) ______

Write out, word for word, the selected verse(s) for each translation

Translation & Verses

Observations

Summary & Conclusions

Application in My Life

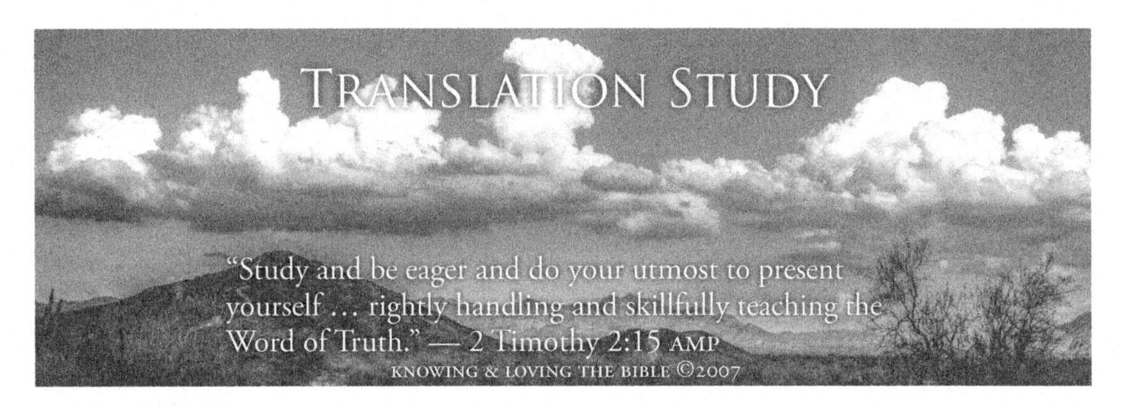

Selected Verse(s) ____

Write out, word for word, the selected verse(s) for each translation

Translation & Verses

Observations

Summary & Conclusions

Application in My Life

Selected Verse(s) ______________________________

Write out, word for word, the selected verse(s) for each translation

Translation & Verses

Observations

Summary & Conclusions

Application in My Life

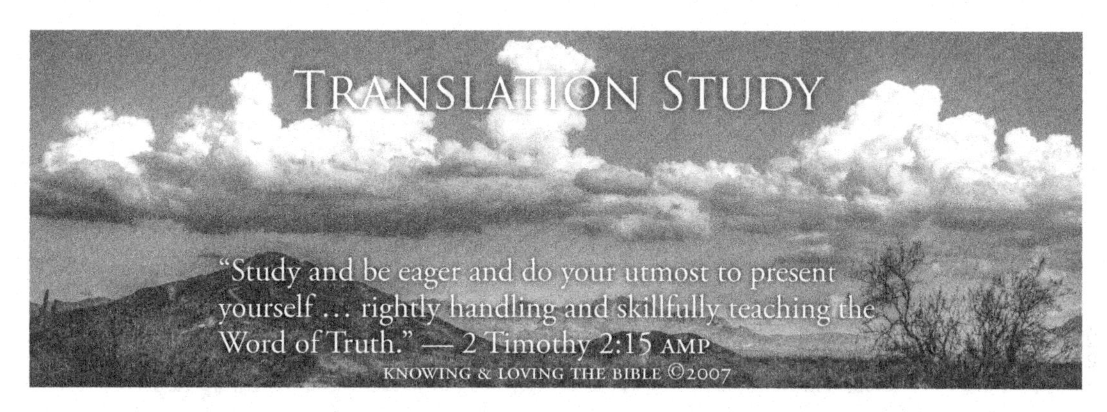

Selected Verse(s) ____

Write out, word for word, the selected verse(s) for each translation

Translation & Verses

Observations

Summary & Conclusions

Application in My Life

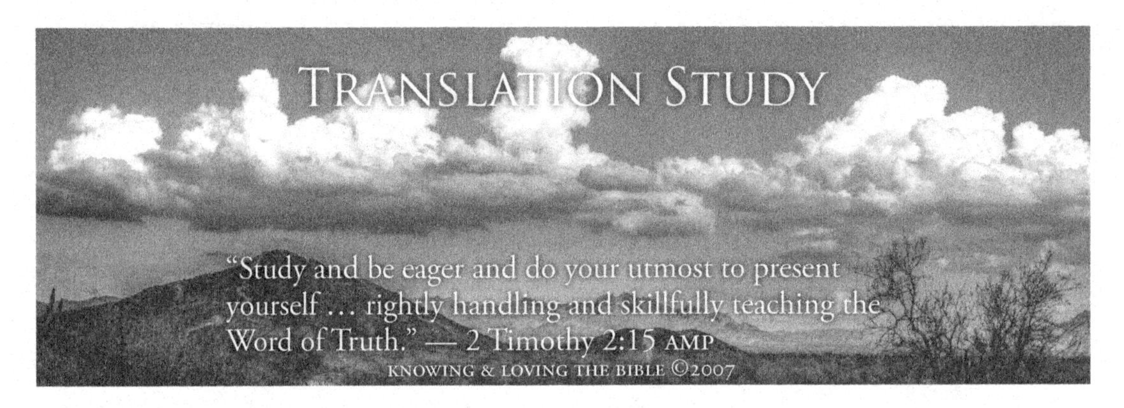

Selected Verse(s) ______________________________

Write out, word for word, the selected verse(s) for each translation

Translation & Verses

Observations

Summary & Conclusions

Application in My Life

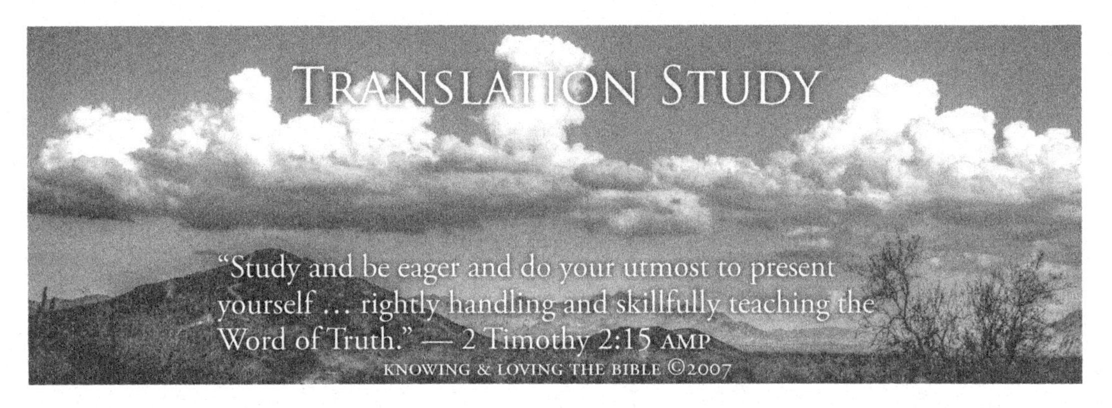

Selected Verse(s) ______________________________

Write out, word for word, the selected verse(s) for each translation

Translation & Verses

Observations

Summary & Conclusions

Application in My Life

Selected Verse(s) ______________________________

Write out, word for word, the selected verse(s) for each translation

Translation & Verses

Observations

Summary & Conclusions

Application in My Life

Selected Verse(s) ______________________________

Write out, word for word, the selected verse(s) for each translation

Translation & Verses

Observations

Summary & Conclusions

Application in My Life

Selected Verse(s) ____________________

Write out, word for word, the selected verse(s) for each translation

Translation & Verses

Observations

Summary & Conclusions

Application in My Life

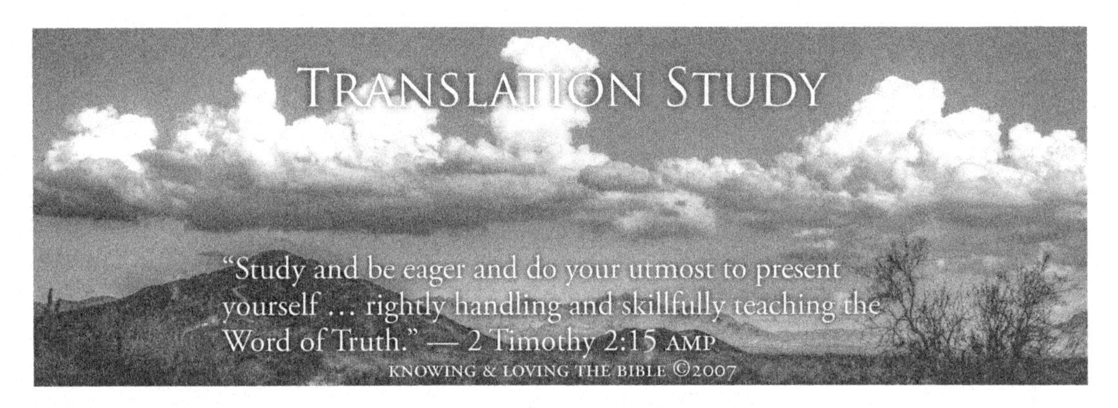

Selected Verse(s) ______________________________

Write out, word for word, the selected verse(s) for each translation

Translation & Verses

Observations

Summary & Conclusions

Application in My Life

Selected Verse(s) ______________________________

Write out, word for word, the selected verse(s) for each translation

Translation & Verses

Observations

Summary & Conclusions

Application in My Life

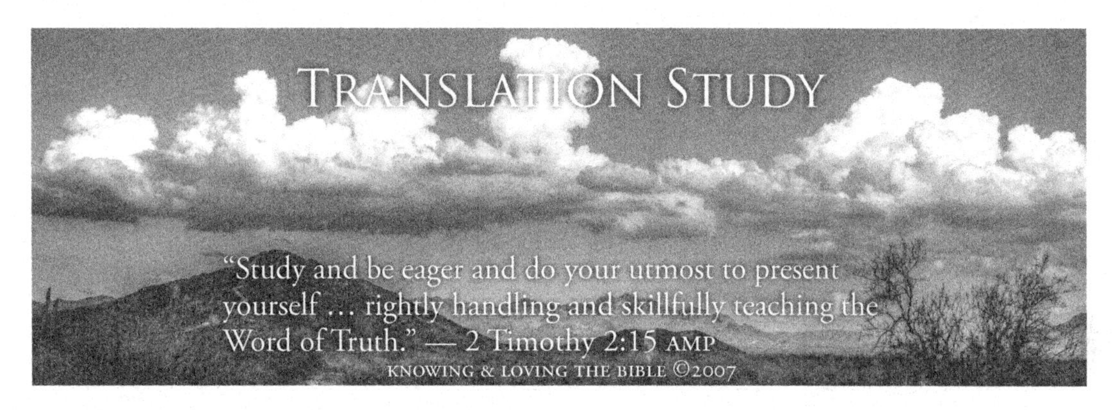

Selected Verse(s) ______________________________

Write out, word for word, the selected verse(s) for each translation

Translation & Verses

Observations

Summary & Conclusions

Application in My Life

Selected Verse(s) ____

Write out, word for word, the selected verse(s) for each translation

Translation & Verses

Observations

Summary & Conclusions

Application in My Life

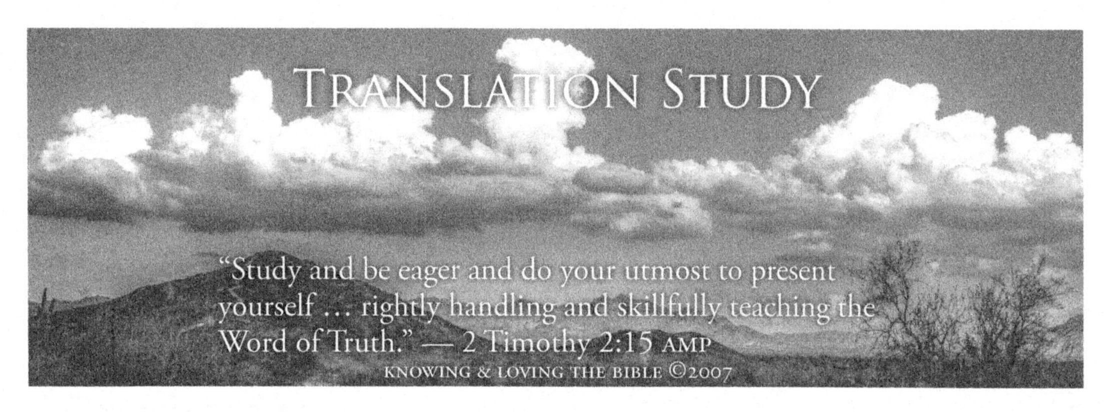

Selected Verse(s) ________________________________

Write out, word for word, the selected verse(s) for each translation

Translation & Verses

Observations

Summary & Conclusions

Application in My Life

Selected Verse(s) ______________________________

Write out, word for word, the selected verse(s) for each translation

Translation & Verses

Observations

Summary & Conclusions

Application in My Life

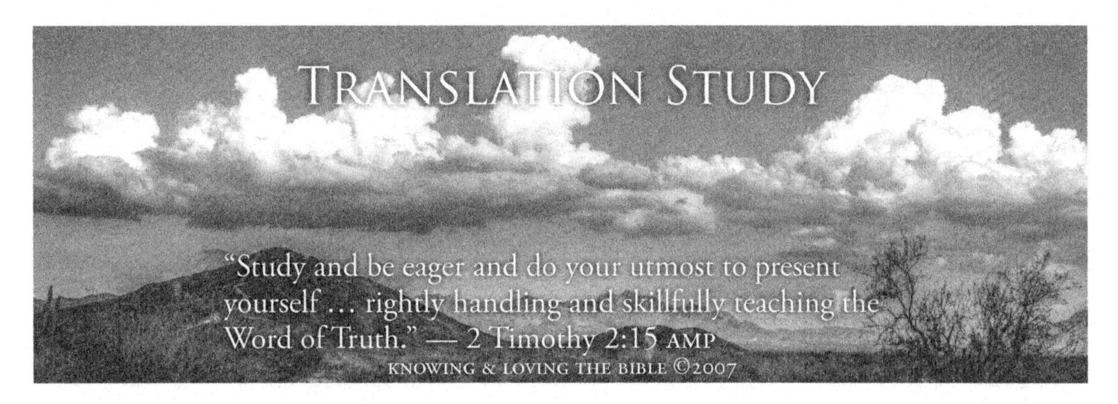

Selected Verse(s) ______________________________

Write out, word for word, the selected verse(s) for each translation

Translation & Verses

Observations

Summary & Conclusions

Application in My Life

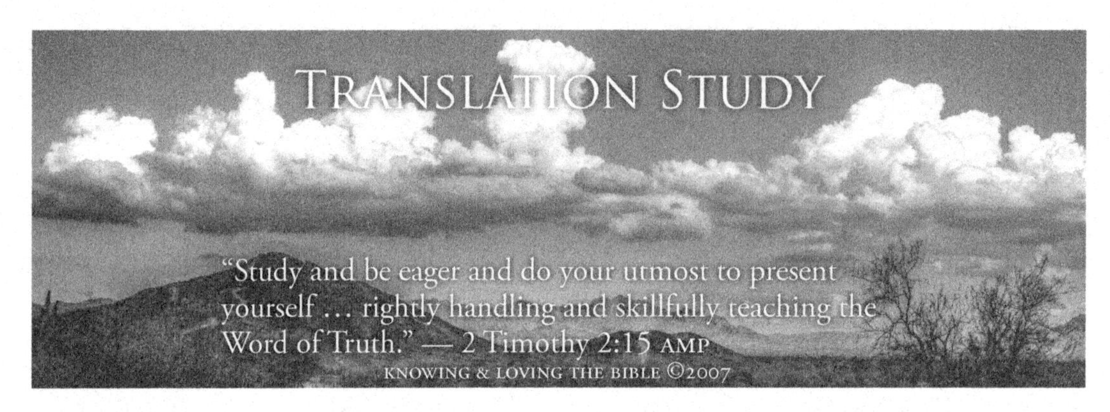

Selected Verse(s) ______________________________

Write out, word for word, the selected verse(s) for each translation

Translation & Verses

Observations

Summary & Conclusions

Application in My Life

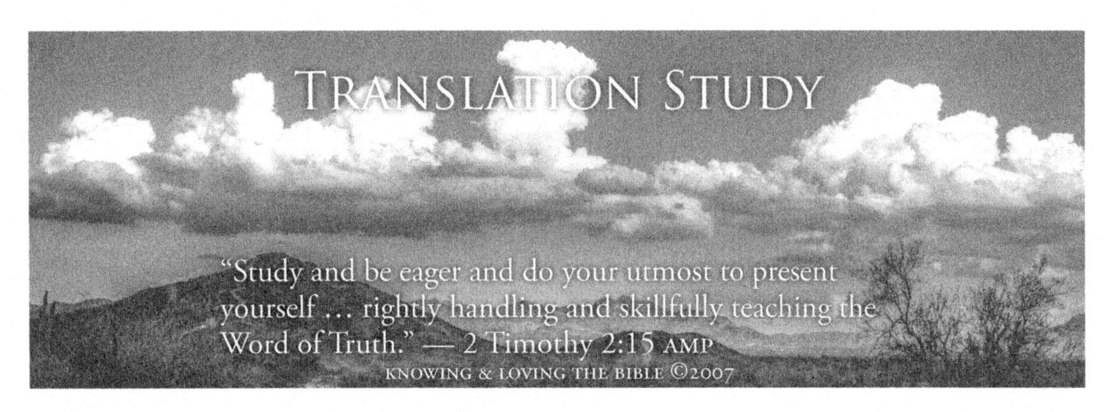

Selected Verse(s) ______________________________

Write out, word for word, the selected verse(s) for each translation

Translation & Verses

Observations

Summary & Conclusions

Application in My Life

Selected Verse(s) ______________________

Write out, word for word, the selected verse(s) for each translation

Translation & Verses

Observations

Summary & Conclusions

Application in My Life

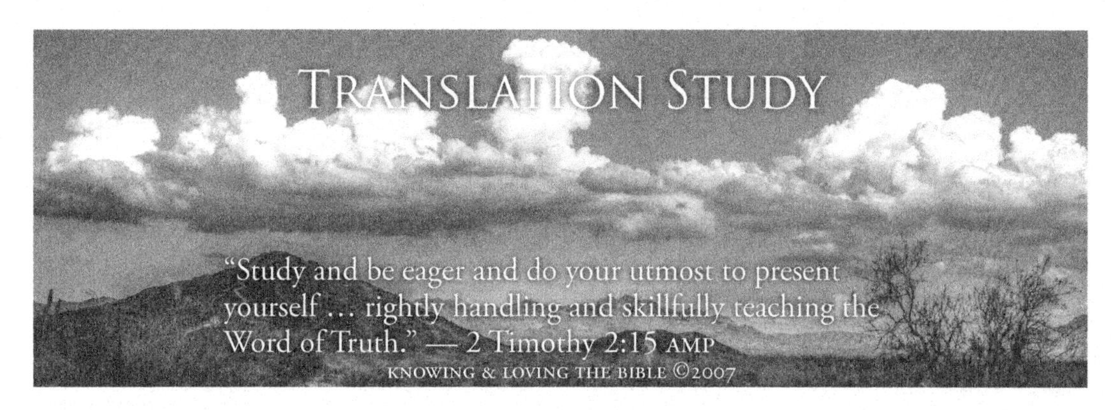

Selected Verse(s) ______________________________

Write out, word for word, the selected verse(s) for each translation

Translation & Verses

Observations

Summary & Conclusions

Application in My Life

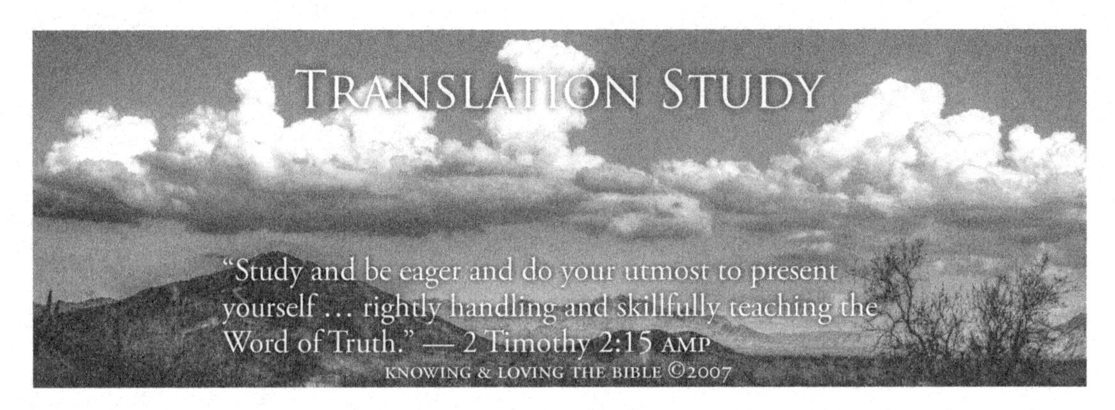

Selected Verse(s) ______________________________

Write out, word for word, the selected verse(s) for each translation

Translation & Verses

Observations

Summary & Conclusions

Application in My Life

Verse–Passage

Word(s):
Strong's #:
Source:
Hebrew–Greek:
Meaning:

Word(s):
Strong's #:
Source:
Hebrew–Greek:
Meaning:

Word(s):
Strong's #:
Source:
Hebrew–Greek:
Meaning:

Word(s):
Strong's #:
Source:
Hebrew–Greek:
Meaning:

Summary & Conclusions

Application in My Life

Verse–Passage

Word(s): Strong's #:
Source: Hebrew–Greek:
Meaning:

Word(s): Strong's #:
Source: Hebrew–Greek:
Meaning:

Word(s): Strong's #:
Source: Hebrew–Greek:
Meaning:

Word(s): Strong's #:
Source: Hebrew–Greek:
Meaning:

Summary & Conclusions

Application in My Life

Verse–Passage

Word(s): Strong's #:
Source: Hebrew–Greek:
Meaning:

Word(s): Strong's #:
Source: Hebrew–Greek:
Meaning:

Word(s): Strong's #:
Source: Hebrew–Greek:
Meaning:

Word(s): Strong's #:
Source: Hebrew–Greek:
Meaning:

Summary & Conclusions

Application in My Life

Verse–Passage

Word(s):
Source:
Meaning:

Strong's #:
Hebrew–Greek:

Word(s):
Source:
Meaning:

Strong's #:
Hebrew–Greek:

Word(s):
Source:
Meaning:

Strong's #:
Hebrew–Greek:

Word(s):
Source:
Meaning:

Strong's #:
Hebrew–Greek:

Summary & Conclusions

Application in My Life

VERSE STUDY

"For the word of God is living and active ..."
— Hebrews 4:12 NASB

Verse–Passage

Word(s): Strong's #:
Source: Hebrew–Greek:
Meaning:

Word(s): Strong's #:
Source: Hebrew–Greek:
Meaning:

Word(s): Strong's #:
Source: Hebrew–Greek:
Meaning:

Word(s): Strong's #:
Source: Hebrew–Greek:
Meaning:

Summary & Conclusions

Application in My Life

Verse–Passage

Word(s): Strong's #:
Source: Hebrew–Greek:
Meaning:

Word(s): Strong's #:
Source: Hebrew–Greek:
Meaning:

Word(s): Strong's #:
Source: Hebrew–Greek:
Meaning:

Word(s): Strong's #:
Source: Hebrew–Greek:
Meaning:

Summary & Conclusions

Application in My Life

Verse–Passage

Word(s): Strong's #:
Source: Hebrew–Greek:
Meaning:

Word(s): Strong's #:
Source: Hebrew–Greek:
Meaning:

Word(s): Strong's #:
Source: Hebrew–Greek:
Meaning:

Word(s): Strong's #:
Source: Hebrew–Greek:
Meaning:

Summary & Conclusions

Application in My Life

Verse–Passage

Word(s): Strong's #:
Source: Hebrew–Greek:
Meaning:

Word(s): Strong's #:
Source: Hebrew–Greek:
Meaning:

Word(s): Strong's #:
Source: Hebrew–Greek:
Meaning:

Word(s): Strong's #:
Source: Hebrew–Greek:
Meaning:

Summary & Conclusions

Application in My Life

Verse–Passage

Word(s): Strong's #:
Source: Hebrew–Greek:
Meaning:

Word(s): Strong's #:
Source: Hebrew–Greek:
Meaning:

Word(s): Strong's #:
Source: Hebrew–Greek:
Meaning:

Word(s): Strong's #:
Source: Hebrew–Greek:
Meaning:

Summary & Conclusions

Application in My Life

Verse–Passage

Word(s):
Source:
Meaning:

Strong's #:
Hebrew–Greek:

Word(s):
Source:
Meaning:

Strong's #:
Hebrew–Greek:

Word(s):
Source:
Meaning:

Strong's #:
Hebrew–Greek:

Word(s):
Source:
Meaning:

Strong's #:
Hebrew–Greek:

Summary & Conclusions

Application in My Life

Verse–Passage

Word(s): Strong's #:
Source: Hebrew–Greek:
Meaning:

Word(s): Strong's #:
Source: Hebrew–Greek:
Meaning:

Word(s): Strong's #:
Source: Hebrew–Greek:
Meaning:

Word(s): Strong's #:
Source: Hebrew–Greek:
Meaning:

Summary & Conclusions

Application in My Life

Verse–Passage

Word(s): Strong's #:
Source: Hebrew–Greek:
Meaning:

Word(s): Strong's #:
Source: Hebrew–Greek:
Meaning:

Word(s): Strong's #:
Source: Hebrew–Greek:
Meaning:

Word(s): Strong's #:
Source: Hebrew–Greek:
Meaning:

Summary & Conclusions

Application in My Life

Verse–Passage

Word(s):
Source:
Meaning:

Strong's #:
Hebrew–Greek:

Word(s):
Source:
Meaning:

Strong's #:
Hebrew–Greek:

Word(s):
Source:
Meaning:

Strong's #:
Hebrew–Greek:

Word(s):
Source:
Meaning:

Strong's #:
Hebrew–Greek:

Summary & Conclusions

Application in My Life

Verse–Passage

Word(s): Strong's #:
Source: Hebrew–Greek:
Meaning:

Word(s): Strong's #:
Source: Hebrew–Greek:
Meaning:

Word(s): Strong's #:
Source: Hebrew–Greek:
Meaning:

Word(s): Strong's #:
Source: Hebrew–Greek:
Meaning:

Summary & Conclusions

Application in My Life

Verse Study

"For the word of God is living and active . . ."
— Hebrews 4:12 NASB

Verse–Passage

Word(s):
Source:
Meaning:

Strong's #:
Hebrew–Greek:

Word(s):
Source:
Meaning:

Strong's #:
Hebrew–Greek:

Word(s):
Source:
Meaning:

Strong's #:
Hebrew–Greek:

Word(s):
Source:
Meaning:

Strong's #:
Hebrew–Greek:

Summary & Conclusions

Application in My Life

Verse–Passage

Word(s):
Source:
Meaning:

Strong's #:
Hebrew–Greek:

Word(s):
Source:
Meaning:

Strong's #:
Hebrew–Greek:

Word(s):
Source:
Meaning:

Strong's #:
Hebrew–Greek:

Word(s):
Source:
Meaning:

Strong's #:
Hebrew–Greek:

Summary & Conclusions

Application in My Life

Verse–Passage

Word(s):
Source:
Meaning:

Strong's #:
Hebrew–Greek:

Word(s):
Source:
Meaning:

Strong's #:
Hebrew–Greek:

Word(s):
Source:
Meaning:

Strong's #:
Hebrew–Greek:

Word(s):
Source:
Meaning:

Strong's #:
Hebrew–Greek:

Summary & Conclusions

Application in My Life

Verse–Passage

Word(s): Strong's #:
Source: Hebrew–Greek:
Meaning:

Word(s): Strong's #:
Source: Hebrew–Greek:
Meaning:

Word(s): Strong's #:
Source: Hebrew–Greek:
Meaning:

Word(s): Strong's #:
Source: Hebrew–Greek:
Meaning:

Summary & Conclusions

Application in My Life

Verse–Passage

Word(s): Strong's #:
Source: Hebrew–Greek:
Meaning:

Word(s): Strong's #:
Source: Hebrew–Greek:
Meaning:

Word(s): Strong's #:
Source: Hebrew–Greek:
Meaning:

Word(s): Strong's #:
Source: Hebrew–Greek:
Meaning:

Summary & Conclusions

Application in My Life

Verse–Passage

Word(s): Strong's #:
Source: Hebrew–Greek:
Meaning:

Word(s): Strong's #:
Source: Hebrew–Greek:
Meaning:

Word(s): Strong's #:
Source: Hebrew–Greek:
Meaning:

Word(s): Strong's #:
Source: Hebrew–Greek:
Meaning:

Summary & Conclusions

Application in My Life

Verse–Passage

Word(s): Strong's #:
Source: Hebrew–Greek:
Meaning:

Word(s): Strong's #:
Source: Hebrew–Greek:
Meaning:

Word(s): Strong's #:
Source: Hebrew–Greek:
Meaning:

Word(s): Strong's #:
Source: Hebrew–Greek:
Meaning:

Summary & Conclusions

Application in My Life

Verse–Passage

Word(s): Strong's #:
Source: Hebrew–Greek:
Meaning:

Word(s): Strong's #:
Source: Hebrew–Greek:
Meaning:

Word(s): Strong's #:
Source: Hebrew–Greek:
Meaning:

Word(s): Strong's #:
Source: Hebrew–Greek:
Meaning:

Summary & Conclusions

Application in My Life

Verse Study

"For the word of God is living and active ..."
— Hebrews 4:12 NASB

Verse–Passage

Word(s):
Source:
Meaning:

Strong's #:
Hebrew–Greek:

Word(s):
Source:
Meaning:

Strong's #:
Hebrew–Greek:

Word(s):
Source:
Meaning:

Strong's #:
Hebrew–Greek:

Word(s):
Source:
Meaning:

Strong's #:
Hebrew–Greek:

Summary & Conclusions

Application in My Life

Verse–Passage

Word(s): Strong's #:
Source: Hebrew–Greek:
Meaning:

Word(s): Strong's #:
Source: Hebrew–Greek:
Meaning:

Word(s): Strong's #:
Source: Hebrew–Greek:
Meaning:

Word(s): Strong's #:
Source: Hebrew–Greek:
Meaning:

Summary & Conclusions

Application in My Life

Verse–Passage

Word(s): Strong's #:
Source: Hebrew–Greek:
Meaning:

Word(s): Strong's #:
Source: Hebrew–Greek:
Meaning:

Word(s): Strong's #:
Source: Hebrew–Greek:
Meaning:

Word(s): Strong's #:
Source: Hebrew–Greek:
Meaning:

Summary & Conclusions

Application in My Life

Verse–Passage

Word(s): Strong's #:
Source: Hebrew–Greek:
Meaning:

Word(s): Strong's #:
Source: Hebrew–Greek:
Meaning:

Word(s): Strong's #:
Source: Hebrew–Greek:
Meaning:

Word(s): Strong's #:
Source: Hebrew–Greek:
Meaning:

Summary & Conclusions

Application in My Life

Verse Study

"For the word of God is living and active ..."
— Hebrews 4:12 NASB

Verse–Passage

Word(s): Strong's #:
Source: Hebrew–Greek:
Meaning:

Word(s): Strong's #:
Source: Hebrew–Greek:
Meaning:

Word(s): Strong's #:
Source: Hebrew–Greek:
Meaning:

Word(s): Strong's #:
Source: Hebrew–Greek:
Meaning:

Summary & Conclusions

Application in My Life

Verse–Passage

Word(s): Strong's #:
Source: Hebrew–Greek:
Meaning:

Word(s): Strong's #:
Source: Hebrew–Greek:
Meaning:

Word(s): Strong's #:
Source: Hebrew–Greek:
Meaning:

Word(s): Strong's #:
Source: Hebrew–Greek:
Meaning:

Summary & Conclusions

Application in My Life

Verse–Passage

Word(s): Strong's #:
Source: Hebrew–Greek:
Meaning:

Word(s): Strong's #:
Source: Hebrew–Greek:
Meaning:

Word(s): Strong's #:
Source: Hebrew–Greek:
Meaning:

Word(s): Strong's #:
Source: Hebrew–Greek:
Meaning:

Summary & Conclusions

Application in My Life

Verse–Passage

Word(s): Strong's #:
Source: Hebrew–Greek:
Meaning:

Word(s): Strong's #:
Source: Hebrew–Greek:
Meaning:

Word(s): Strong's #:
Source: Hebrew–Greek:
Meaning:

Word(s): Strong's #:
Source: Hebrew–Greek:
Meaning:

Summary & Conclusions

Application in My Life

Word(s):
Other Translations:
Scripture Passage for Word(s):

Strong's #:
Hebrew–Greek:

Strong's Concordance

Vine's Expository Dictionary

Key Word Study Bible, Complete Word Study NT&OT, Theological WB OT, Dictionaries

Linguistic Key To The Greek NT, Wuest's Word Studies, Brown's Dictionary of NT Theology, Robertson's Word Pictures, Commentaries

Other Uses in Immediate Area of Study

Other Uses in Old & New Testament

Summary & Conclusions

Meaning in Present Study

Application in My Life

Word(s):

Strong's #:

Other Translations:

Hebrew–Greek:

Scripture Passage for Word(s):

Strong's Concordance

Vine's Expository Dictionary

Key Word Study Bible, Complete Word Study NT&OT, Theological WB OT, Dictionaries

Linguistic Key To The Greek NT, Wuest's Word Studies, Brown's Dictionary of NT Theology, Robertson's Word Pictures, Commentaries

Other Uses in Immediate Area of Study

Other Uses in Old & New Testament

Summary & Conclusions

Meaning in Present Study

Application in My Life

Word(s):

Strong's #:

Other Translations:

Hebrew–Greek:

Scripture Passage for Word(s):

Strong's Concordance

Vine's Expository Dictionary

Key Word Study Bible, Complete Word Study NT&OT, Theological WB OT, Dictionaries

Linguistic Key To The Greek NT, Wuest's Word Studies, Brown's Dictionary of NT Theology, Robertson's Word Pictures, Commentaries

Other Uses in Immediate Area of Study

Other Uses in Old & New Testament

Summary & Conclusions

Meaning in Present Study

Application in My Life

Word(s):
Other Translations:
Scripture Passage for Word(s):

Strong's #:
Hebrew–Greek:

Strong's Concordance

Vine's Expository Dictionary

Key Word Study Bible, Complete Word Study NT&OT, Theological WB OT, Dictionaries

Linguistic Key To The Greek NT, Wuest's Word Studies, Brown's Dictionary of NT Theology, Robertson's Word Pictures, Commentaries

Other Uses in Immediate Area of Study

Other Uses in Old & New Testament

Summary & Conclusions

Meaning in Present Study

Application in My Life

Word(s):

Strong's #:

Other Translations:

Hebrew–Greek:

Scripture Passage for Word(s):

Strong's Concordance

Vine's Expository Dictionary

Key Word Study Bible, Complete Word Study NT&OT, Theological WB OT, Dictionaries

Linguistic Key To The Greek NT, Wuest's Word Studies, Brown's Dictionary of NT Theology, Robertson's Word Pictures, Commentaries

Other Uses in Immediate Area of Study

Other Uses in Old & New Testament

Summary & Conclusions

Meaning in Present Study

Application in My Life

Word(s): Strong's #:

Other Translations: Hebrew–Greek:

Scripture Passage for Word(s):

Strong's Concordance

Vine's Expository Dictionary

Key Word Study Bible, Complete Word Study NT&OT, Theological WB OT, Dictionaries

Linguistic Key To The Greek NT, Wuest's Word Studies, Brown's Dictionary of NT Theology, Robertson's Word Pictures, Commentaries

Other Uses in Immediate Area of Study

Other Uses in Old & New Testament

Summary & Conclusions

Meaning in Present Study

Application in My Life

Word(s):
Other Translations:
Scripture Passage for Word(s):

Strong's #:
Hebrew–Greek:

Strong's Concordance

Vine's Expository Dictionary

Key Word Study Bible, Complete Word Study NT&OT, Theological WB OT, Dictionaries

Linguistic Key To The Greek NT, Wuest's Word Studies, Brown's Dictionary of NT Theology, Robertson's Word Pictures, Commentaries

Other Uses in Immediate Area of Study

Other Uses in Old & New Testament

Summary & Conclusions

Meaning in Present Study

Application in My Life

Word(s): Strong's #:

Other Translations: Hebrew–Greek:

Scripture Passage for Word(s):

Strong's Concordance

Vine's Expository Dictionary

Key Word Study Bible, Complete Word Study NT&OT, Theological WB OT, Dictionaries

Linguistic Key To The Greek NT, Wuest's Word Studies, Brown's Dictionary of NT Theology, Robertson's Word Pictures, Commentaries

Other Uses in Immediate Area of Study

Other Uses in Old & New Testament

Summary & Conclusions

Meaning in Present Study

Application in My Life

Word(s): Strong's #:
Other Translations: Hebrew–Greek:
Scripture Passage for Word(s):

Strong's Concordance

Vine's Expository Dictionary

Key Word Study Bible, Complete Word Study NT&OT, Theological WB OT, Dictionaries

Linguistic Key To The Greek NT, Wuest's Word Studies, Brown's Dictionary of NT Theology, Robertson's Word Pictures, Commentaries

Other Uses in Immediate Area of Study

Other Uses in Old & New Testament

Summary & Conclusions

Meaning in Present Study

Application in My Life

Word(s):
Other Translations:
Scripture Passage for Word(s):

Strong's #:
Hebrew–Greek:

Strong's Concordance

Vine's Expository Dictionary

Key Word Study Bible, Complete Word Study NT&OT, Theological WB OT, Dictionaries

Linguistic Key To The Greek NT, Wuest's Word Studies, Brown's Dictionary of NT Theology, Robertson's Word Pictures, Commentaries

Other Uses in Immediate Area of Study

Other Uses in Old & New Testament

Summary & Conclusions

Meaning in Present Study

Application in My Life

Word(s):

Strong's #:

Other Translations:

Hebrew–Greek:

Scripture Passage for Word(s):

Strong's Concordance

Vine's Expository Dictionary

Key Word Study Bible, Complete Word Study NT&OT, Theological WB OT, Dictionaries

Linguistic Key To The Greek NT, Wuest's Word Studies, Brown's Dictionary of NT Theology, Robertson's Word Pictures, Commentaries

Other Uses in Immediate Area of Study

Other Uses in Old & New Testament

Summary & Conclusions

Meaning in Present Study

Application in My Life

Word(s):
Other Translations:
Scripture Passage for Word(s):

Strong's #:
Hebrew–Greek:

Strong's Concordance

Vine's Expository Dictionary

Key Word Study Bible, Complete Word Study NT&OT, Theological WB OT, Dictionaries

Linguistic Key To The Greek NT, Wuest's Word Studies, Brown's Dictionary of NT Theology, Robertson's Word Pictures, Commentaries

Other Uses in Immediate Area of Study

Other Uses in Old & New Testament

Summary & Conclusions

Meaning in Present Study

Application in My Life

Word(s):

Strong's #:

Other Translations:

Hebrew–Greek:

Scripture Passage for Word(s):

Strong's Concordance

Vine's Expository Dictionary

Key Word Study Bible, Complete Word Study NT&OT, Theological WB OT, Dictionaries

Linguistic Key To The Greek NT, Wuest's Word Studies, Brown's Dictionary of NT Theology, Robertson's Word Pictures, Commentaries

Other Uses in Immediate Area of Study

Other Uses in Old & New Testament

Summary & Conclusions

Meaning in Present Study

Application in My Life

Word(s):
Strong's #:
Other Translations:
Hebrew–Greek:
Scripture Passage for Word(s):

Strong's Concordance

Vine's Expository Dictionary

Key Word Study Bible, Complete Word Study NT&OT, Theological WB OT, Dictionaries

Linguistic Key To The Greek NT, Wuest's Word Studies, Brown's Dictionary of NT Theology, Robertson's Word Pictures, Commentaries

Other Uses in Immediate Area of Study

Other Uses in Old & New Testament

Summary & Conclusions

Meaning in Present Study

Application in My Life

Word(s):
Other Translations:
Scripture Passage for Word(s):

Strong's #:
Hebrew–Greek:

Strong's Concordance

Vine's Expository Dictionary

Key Word Study Bible, Complete Word Study NT&OT, Theological WB OT, Dictionaries

Linguistic Key To The Greek NT, Wuest's Word Studies, Brown's Dictionary of NT Theology, Robertson's Word Pictures, Commentaries

Other Uses in Immediate Area of Study

Other Uses in Old & New Testament

Summary & Conclusions

Meaning in Present Study

Application in My Life

Word(s):
Strong's #:
Other Translations:
Hebrew–Greek:
Scripture Passage for Word(s):

Strong's Concordance

Vine's Expository Dictionary

Key Word Study Bible, Complete Word Study NT&OT, Theological WB OT, Dictionaries

Linguistic Key To The Greek NT, Wuest's Word Studies, Brown's Dictionary of NT Theology, Robertson's Word Pictures, Commentaries

Other Uses in Immediate Area of Study

Other Uses in Old & New Testament

Summary & Conclusions

Meaning in Present Study

Application in My Life

Word(s): Strong's #:

Other Translations: Hebrew–Greek:

Scripture Passage for Word(s):

Strong's Concordance

Vine's Expository Dictionary

Key Word Study Bible, Complete Word Study NT&OT, Theological WB OT, Dictionaries

Linguistic Key To The Greek NT, Wuest's Word Studies, Brown's Dictionary of NT Theology, Robertson's Word Pictures, Commentaries

Other Uses in Immediate Area of Study

Other Uses in Old & New Testament

Summary & Conclusions

Meaning in Present Study

Application in My Life

Word(s):

Strong's #:

Other Translations:

Hebrew–Greek:

Scripture Passage for Word(s):

Strong's Concordance

Vine's Expository Dictionary

Key Word Study Bible, Complete Word Study NT&OT, Theological WB OT, Dictionaries

Linguistic Key To The Greek NT, Wuest's Word Studies, Brown's Dictionary of NT Theology, Robertson's Word Pictures, Commentaries

Other Uses in Immediate Area of Study

Other Uses in Old & New Testament

Summary & Conclusions

Meaning in Present Study

Application in My Life

Word(s):
Other Translations:
Scripture Passage for Word(s):

Strong's #:
Hebrew–Greek:

Strong's Concordance

Vine's Expository Dictionary

Key Word Study Bible, Complete Word Study NT&OT, Theological WB OT, Dictionaries

Linguistic Key To The Greek NT, Wuest's Word Studies, Brown's Dictionary of NT Theology, Robertson's Word Pictures, Commentaries

Other Uses in Immediate Area of Study

Other Uses in Old & New Testament

Summary & Conclusions

Meaning in Present Study

Application in My Life

Word(s):

Strong's #:

Other Translations:

Hebrew–Greek:

Scripture Passage for Word(s):

Strong's Concordance

Vine's Expository Dictionary

Key Word Study Bible, Complete Word Study NT&OT, Theological WB OT, Dictionaries

Linguistic Key To The Greek NT, Wuest's Word Studies, Brown's Dictionary of NT Theology, Robertson's Word Pictures, Commentaries

Other Uses in Immediate Area of Study

Other Uses in Old & New Testament

Summary & Conclusions

Meaning in Present Study

Application in My Life

Reference Study

PAGE ONE

"...the grass withers and the flowers fall but the word of the Lord stands forever." — 1 Peter 1:24-25 NIV

Verse–Topic ____________________ *Scripture* ____________________

Record observations and insights from the following references related to the selected verse or topic. Define any key words.

Key Words–Definitions

____

Reference

____

Reference

____

Reference

____

Reference

Reference

Reference

Reference

Reference

Summary–Conclusions

Application in My Life

REFERENCE STUDY

PAGE ONE

"…the grass withers and the flowers fall but the word of the Lord stands forever." — 1 Peter 1:24-25 NIV

Verse–Topic ____________________ *Scripture* ____________________

Record observations and insights from the following references related to the selected verse or topic. Define any key words.

Key Words–Definitions

____

Reference

____

Reference

____

Reference

____

Reference

Reference

Reference

Reference

Reference

Summary–Conclusions

Application in My Life

Reference Study

PAGE ONE

"...the grass withers and the flowers fall but the word of the Lord stands forever." — 1 Peter 1:24-25 NIV

Verse–Topic ______________________ *Scripture* ______________________________

Record observations and insights from the following references related to the selected verse or topic. Define any key words.

Key Words–Definitions

____

Reference

____

Reference

____

Reference

____

Reference

Reference

Reference

Reference

Reference

Summary–Conclusions

Application in My Life

Reference Study

PAGE ONE

"...the grass withers and the flowers fall but the word of the Lord stands forever." — 1 Peter 1:24-25 NIV

Verse–Topic ____________________ *Scripture* ____________________

Record observations and insights from the following references related to the selected verse or topic. Define any key words.

Key Words–Definitions

____

Reference

____

Reference

____

Reference

____

Reference

Reference

Reference

Reference

Reference

Summary–Conclusions

Application in My Life

Reference Study

PAGE ONE

"...the grass withers and the flowers fall but the word of the Lord stands forever." — 1 Peter 1:24-25 NIV

Verse–Topic ____________________ *Scripture* ____________________

Record observations and insights from the following references related to the selected verse or topic. Define any key words.

Key Words–Definitions

____

Reference

____

Reference

____

Reference

____

Reference

Reference Study

Page Two

Reference

Reference

Reference

Reference

Summary–Conclusions

Application in My Life

Reference Study

PAGE ONE

"…the grass withers and the flowers fall but the word of the Lord stands forever." — 1 Peter 1:24-25 NIV

Verse–Topic ____________________ *Scripture* ______________________________

Record observations and insights from the following references related to the selected verse or topic. Define any key words.

Key Words–Definitions

____

Reference

____

Reference

____

Reference

____

Reference

Reference

Reference

Reference

Reference

Summary–Conclusions

Application in My Life

Reference Study

PAGE ONE

"...the grass withers and the flowers fall but the word of the Lord stands forever." — 1 Peter 1:24-25 NIV

Verse–Topic ____________________ *Scripture* ______________________________

Record observations and insights from the following references related to the selected verse or topic. Define any key words.

Key Words–Definitions

____

Reference

____

Reference

____

Reference

____

Reference

Reference

Reference

Reference

Reference

Summary–Conclusions

Application in My Life

Reference Study

PAGE ONE

"...the grass withers and the flowers fall but the word of the Lord stands forever." — 1 Peter 1:24-25 NIV

Verse–Topic ____________________ *Scripture* ____________________

Record observations and insights from the following references related to the selected verse or topic. Define any key words.

Key Words–Definitions

____

Reference

____

Reference

____

Reference

____

Reference

Reference

Reference

Reference

Reference

Summary–Conclusions

Application in My Life

Reference Study

PAGE ONE

"...the grass withers and the flowers fall but the word of the Lord stands forever." — 1 Peter 1:24-25 NIV

Verse–Topic ____________________ *Scripture* ______________________________

Record observations and insights from the following references related to the selected verse or topic. Define any key words.

Key Words–Definitions

____

Reference

____

Reference

____

Reference

____

Reference

Reference

Reference

Reference

Reference

Summary–Conclusions

Application in My Life

Reference Study

PAGE ONE

"...the grass withers and the flowers fall but the word of the Lord stands forever." — 1 Peter 1:24-25 NIV

Verse–Topic ____________________ *Scripture* ______________________________

Record observations and insights from the following references related to the selected verse or topic. Define any key words.

Key Words–Definitions

____

Reference

____

Reference

____

Reference

____

Reference

Reference

Reference

Reference

Reference

Summary–Conclusions

Application in My Life

REFERENCE STUDY

PAGE ONE

"...the grass withers and the flowers fall but the word of the Lord stands forever." — 1 Peter 1:24-25 NIV

Verse–Topic ____________________ *Scripture* ____________________________

Record observations and insights from the following references related to the selected verse or topic. Define any key words.

Key Words–Definitions

____

Reference

____

Reference

____

Reference

____

Reference

Reference

Reference

Reference

Reference

Summary–Conclusions

Application in My Life

Reference Study

PAGE ONE

"...the grass withers and the flowers fall but the word of the Lord stands forever." — 1 Peter 1:24-25 NIV

Verse–Topic ____________________ *Scripture* ____________________

Record observations and insights from the following references related to the selected verse or topic. Define any key words.

Key Words–Definitions

____

Reference

____

Reference

____

Reference

____

Reference

REFERENCE STUDY

PAGE TWO

Reference

Reference

Reference

Reference

Summary–Conclusions

Application in My Life

Reference Study

PAGE ONE

"...the grass withers and the flowers fall but the word of the Lord stands forever." — 1 Peter 1:24-25 NIV

Verse–Topic ______________________ *Scripture* ______________________

Record observations and insights from the following references related to the selected verse or topic. Define any key words.

Key Words–Definitions

____

Reference

____

Reference

____

Reference

____

Reference

Reference

Reference

Reference

Reference

Summary–Conclusions

Application in My Life

REFERENCE STUDY

PAGE ONE

"...the grass withers and the flowers fall but the word of the Lord stands forever." — 1 Peter 1:24-25 NIV

Verse–Topic ____________________ *Scripture* ______________________________

Record observations and insights from the following references related to the selected verse or topic. Define any key words.

Key Words–Definitions

____

Reference

____

Reference

____

Reference

____

Reference

Reference Study

PAGE TWO

Reference

Reference

Reference

Reference

Summary–Conclusions

Application in My Life

Reference Study

PAGE ONE

"...the grass withers and the flowers fall but the word of the Lord stands forever." — 1 Peter 1:24-25 NIV

Verse–Topic ____________________ *Scripture* ____________________

Record observations and insights from the following references related to the selected verse or topic. Define any key words.

Key Words–Definitions

____

Reference

____

Reference

____

Reference

____

Reference

REFERENCE STUDY

PAGE TWO

Reference

Reference

Reference

Reference

Summary–Conclusions

Application in My Life

Reference Study

PAGE ONE

"…the grass withers and the flowers fall but the word of the Lord stands forever." — 1 Peter 1:24-25 NIV

Verse–Topic ______________________ *Scripture* ______________________

Record observations and insights from the following references related to the selected verse or topic. Define any key words.

Key Words–Definitions

____

Reference

____

Reference

____

Reference

____

Reference

Reference

Reference

Reference

Reference

Summary–Conclusions

Application in My Life

Reference Study

PAGE ONE

"…the grass withers and the flowers fall but the word of the Lord stands forever." — 1 Peter 1:24-25 NIV

Verse–Topic ________________ *Scripture* ________________

Record observations and insights from the following references related to the selected verse or topic. Define any key words.

Key Words–Definitions

____

Reference

____

Reference

____

Reference

____

Reference

Reference Study

PAGE TWO

Reference

Reference

Reference

Reference

Summary–Conclusions

Application in My Life

Reference Study

Page One

"...the grass withers and the flowers fall but the word of the Lord stands forever." — 1 Peter 1:24-25 NIV

Verse–Topic ____________________ *Scripture* ______________________________

Record observations and insights from the following references related to the selected verse or topic. Define any key words.

Key Words–Definitions

____

Reference

____

Reference

____

Reference

____

Reference

Reference

Reference

Reference

Reference

Summary–Conclusions

Application in My Life

REFERENCE STUDY

PAGE ONE

"…the grass withers and the flowers fall but the word of the Lord stands forever." — 1 Peter 1:24-25 NIV

Verse–Topic ____________________ *Scripture* ____________________________

Record observations and insights from the following references related to the selected verse or topic. Define any key words.

Key Words–Definitions

____

Reference

____

Reference

____

Reference

____

Reference

REFERENCE STUDY

PAGE TWO

Reference

Reference

Reference

Reference

Summary–Conclusions

Application in My Life

REFERENCE STUDY

PAGE ONE

"...the grass withers and the flowers fall but the word of the Lord stands forever." — 1 Peter 1:24-25 NIV

Verse–Topic ____________________ *Scripture* ____________________

Record observations and insights from the following references related to the selected verse or topic. Define any key words.

Key Words–Definitions

____

Reference

____

Reference

____

Reference

____

Reference

Reference

Reference

Reference

Reference

Summary–Conclusions

Application in My Life

TOPICAL STUDY

PAGE ONE

"...the grass withers and the flowers fall but the word of the Lord stands forever." — 1 Peter 1:24-25 NIV

Verse–Topic ____________________ *Scripture* ____________________

Record observations and insights from the following references related to the selected verse or topic. Define any key words.

Key Words–Definitions

____
Reference

____
Reference

____
Reference

____
Reference

Reference

Reference

Reference

Reference

Summary–Conclusions

Application in My Life

Topical Study

PAGE ONE

"...the grass withers and the flowers fall but the word of the Lord stands forever." — 1 Peter 1:24-25 NIV

Verse–Topic ______________________ *Scripture* ______________________

Record observations and insights from the following references related to the selected verse or topic. Define any key words.

Key Words–Definitions

____

Reference

____

Reference

____

Reference

____

Reference

Reference

Reference

Reference

Reference

Summary–Conclusions

Application in My Life

TOPICAL STUDY

PAGE ONE

"...the grass withers and the flowers fall but the word of the Lord stands forever." — 1 Peter 1:24-25 NIV

Verse–Topic ____________________ *Scripture* ____________________

Record observations and insights from the following references related to the selected verse or topic. Define any key words.

Key Words–Definitions

____

Reference

____

Reference

____

Reference

____

Reference

Reference

Reference

Reference

Reference

Summary–Conclusions

Application in My Life

TOPICAL STUDY

PAGE ONE

"...the grass withers and the flowers fall but the word of the Lord stands forever." — 1 Peter 1:24-25 NIV

Verse–Topic ________________ *Scripture* ________________

Record observations and insights from the following references related to the selected verse or topic. Define any key words.

Key Words–Definitions

____

Reference

____

Reference

____

Reference

____

Reference

Reference

Reference

Reference

Reference

Summary–Conclusions

Application in My Life

TOPICAL STUDY

PAGE ONE

"...the grass withers and the flowers fall but the word of the Lord stands forever." — 1 Peter 1:24-25 NIV

Verse–Topic ____________________ *Scripture* ____________________________

Record observations and insights from the following references related to the selected verse or topic. Define any key words.

Key Words–Definitions

____

Reference

____

Reference

____

Reference

____

Reference

Reference

Reference

Reference

Reference

Summary–Conclusions

Application in My Life

TOPICAL STUDY

PAGE ONE

"…the grass withers and the flowers fall but the word of the Lord stands forever." — 1 Peter 1:24-25 NIV

Verse–Topic ______________________ *Scripture* ______________________________

Record observations and insights from the following references related to the selected verse or topic. Define any key words.

Key Words–Definitions

____

Reference

____

Reference

____

Reference

____

Reference

Reference

Reference

Reference

Reference

Summary–Conclusions

Application in My Life

TOPICAL STUDY

PAGE ONE

"...the grass withers and the flowers fall but the word of the Lord stands forever." — 1 Peter 1:24-25 NIV

Verse–Topic ____________________ *Scripture* ____________________

Record observations and insights from the following references related to the selected verse or topic. Define any key words.

Key Words–Definitions

____
Reference

____
Reference

____
Reference

____
Reference

Reference

Reference

Reference

Reference

Summary–Conclusions

Application in My Life

TOPICAL STUDY

PAGE ONE

"...the grass withers and the flowers fall but the word of the Lord stands forever." — 1 Peter 1:24-25 NIV

Verse–Topic ____________________ *Scripture* ______________________________

Record observations and insights from the following references related to the selected verse or topic. Define any key words.

Key Words–Definitions

____

Reference

____

Reference

____

Reference

____

Reference

Reference

Reference

Reference

Reference

Summary–Conclusions

Application in My Life

TOPICAL STUDY

PAGE ONE

"...the grass withers and the flowers fall but the word of the Lord stands forever." — 1 Peter 1:24-25 NIV

Verse–Topic ____________________ *Scripture* ____________________________

Record observations and insights from the following references related to the selected verse or topic. Define any key words.

Key Words–Definitions

____

Reference

____

Reference

____

Reference

____

Reference

Reference

Reference

Reference

Reference

Summary–Conclusions

Application in My Life

TOPICAL STUDY

PAGE ONE

"...the grass withers and the flowers fall but the word of the Lord stands forever." — 1 Peter 1:24-25 NIV

Verse–Topic ________________ *Scripture* ________________

Record observations and insights from the following references related to the selected verse or topic. Define any key words.

Key Words–Definitions

____

Reference

____

Reference

____

Reference

____

Reference

Reference

Reference

Reference

Reference

Summary–Conclusions

Application in My Life

TOPICAL STUDY

PAGE ONE

"...the grass withers and the flowers fall but the word of the Lord stands forever." — 1 Peter 1:24-25 NIV

Verse–Topic ____________________ *Scripture* ____________________

Record observations and insights from the following references related to the selected verse or topic. Define any key words.

Key Words–Definitions

____

Reference

____

Reference

____

Reference

____

Reference

Reference

Reference

Reference

Reference

Summary–Conclusions

Application in My Life

TOPICAL STUDY

PAGE ONE

"...the grass withers and the flowers fall but the word of the Lord stands forever." — 1 Peter 1:24-25 NIV

Verse–Topic ____________________ *Scripture* ______________________________

Record observations and insights from the following references related to the selected verse or topic. Define any key words.

Key Words–Definitions

____
Reference

____
Reference

____
Reference

____
Reference

Reference

Reference

Reference

Reference

Summary–Conclusions

Application in My Life

TOPICAL STUDY

PAGE ONE

"…the grass withers and the flowers fall but the word of the Lord stands forever." — 1 Peter 1:24-25 NIV

Verse–Topic ____________________ *Scripture* ____________________________

Record observations and insights from the following references related to the selected verse or topic. Define any key words.

Key Words–Definitions

____

Reference

____

Reference

____

Reference

____

Reference

Reference

Reference

Reference

Reference

Summary–Conclusions

Application in My Life

TOPICAL STUDY

PAGE ONE

"...the grass withers and the flowers fall but the word of the Lord stands forever." — 1 Peter 1:24-25 NIV

Verse–Topic ______________________ *Scripture* ______________________

Record observations and insights from the following references related to the selected verse or topic. Define any key words.

Key Words–Definitions

____

Reference

____

Reference

____

Reference

____

Reference

Reference

Reference

Reference

Reference

Summary–Conclusions

Application in My Life

TOPICAL STUDY

PAGE ONE

"...the grass withers and the flowers fall but the word of the Lord stands forever." — 1 Peter 1:24-25 NIV

Verse–Topic ____________________ *Scripture* ____________________

Record observations and insights from the following references related to the selected verse or topic. Define any key words.

Key Words–Definitions

____

Reference

____

Reference

____

Reference

____

Reference

Reference

Reference

Reference

Reference

Summary–Conclusions

Application in My Life

TOPICAL STUDY

PAGE ONE

"...the grass withers and the flowers fall but the word of the Lord stands forever." — 1 Peter 1:24-25 NIV

Verse–Topic ____________________ *Scripture* ______________________________

Record observations and insights from the following references related to the selected verse or topic. Define any key words.

Key Words–Definitions

____

Reference

____

Reference

____

Reference

____

Reference

Reference

Reference

Reference

Reference

Summary–Conclusions

Application in My Life

TOPICAL STUDY

PAGE ONE

"...the grass withers and the flowers fall but the word of the Lord stands forever." — 1 Peter 1:24-25 NIV

Verse–Topic ____________________ *Scripture* ____________________

Record observations and insights from the following references related to the selected verse or topic. Define any key words.

Key Words–Definitions

____

Reference

____

Reference

____

Reference

____

Reference

Reference

Reference

Reference

Reference

Summary–Conclusions

Application in My Life

TOPICAL STUDY

PAGE ONE

"...the grass withers and the flowers fall but the word of the Lord stands forever." — 1 Peter 1:24-25 NIV

Verse–Topic ________________ *Scripture* ________________

Record observations and insights from the following references related to the selected verse or topic. Define any key words.

Key Words–Definitions

____

Reference

____

Reference

____

Reference

____

Reference

Reference

Reference

Reference

Reference

Summary–Conclusions

Application in My Life

TOPICAL STUDY

PAGE ONE

"...the grass withers and the flowers fall but the word of the Lord stands forever." — 1 Peter 1:24-25 NIV

Verse–Topic ____________________ *Scripture* ______________________________

Record observations and insights from the following references related to the selected verse or topic. Define any key words.

Key Words–Definitions

____

Reference

____

Reference

____

Reference

____

Reference

Reference

Reference

Reference

Reference

Summary–Conclusions

Application in My Life

TOPICAL STUDY

PAGE ONE

"...the grass withers and the flowers fall but the word of the Lord stands forever." — 1 Peter 1:24-25 NIV

Verse–Topic ____________________ *Scripture* ____________________

Record observations and insights from the following references related to the selected verse or topic. Define any key words.

Key Words–Definitions

____

Reference

____

Reference

____

Reference

____

Reference

Reference

Reference

Reference

Reference

Summary–Conclusions

Application in My Life

CHARACTER STUDY

PAGE ONE

"... considering the result of their conduct, imitate their faith." — Hebrews 13:7 NASB

Verse–Topic ____________________

Area of Study ______________________________

Key Scripture Passages ____________________________________

Record observations of life, insights of character, important events, relationship with God

Verse & Observations

Significant Observations of Character's Life

Major Character Qualities

Important Life Events

Relationship with God

Information from other Sources

Significant Principles Summary

Application in My Life

Character Study

PAGE ONE

"... considering the result of their conduct, imitate their faith." — Hebrews 13:7 NASB

Verse–Topic ____________________

Area of Study ______________________________

Key Scripture Passages ____________________________________

Record observations of life, insights of character, important events, relationship with God

Verse & Observations

Significant Observations of Character's Life

Major Character Qualities

Important Life Events

Relationship with God

Information from other Sources

Significant Principles Summary

Application in My Life

Character Study

PAGE ONE

"... considering the result of their conduct, imitate their faith." — Hebrews 13:7 NASB

Verse–Topic ____________________

Area of Study ______________________________

Key Scripture Passages ____________________________________

Record observations of life, insights of character, important events, relationship with God

Verse & Observations

Significant Observations of Character's Life

Major Character Qualities

Important Life Events

Relationship with God

Information from other Sources

Significant Principles Summary

Application in My Life

Character Study

Page One

"... considering the result of their conduct, imitate their faith." — Hebrews 13:7 NASB

Verse–Topic ____________________

Area of Study ________________________________

Key Scripture Passages ____

Record observations of life, insights of character, important events, relationship with God

Verse & Observations

Significant Observations of Character's Life

Major Character Qualities

Important Life Events

Relationship with God

Information from other Sources

Significant Principles Summary

Application in My Life

CHARACTER STUDY

PAGE ONE

"... considering the result of their conduct, imitate their faith." — Hebrews 13:7 NASB

Verse–Topic ____________________

Area of Study ______________________________

Key Scripture Passages ____________________________________

Record observations of life, insights of character, important events, relationship with God

Verse & Observations

Significant Observations of Character's Life

Major Character Qualities

Important Life Events

Relationship with God

Information from other Sources

Significant Principles Summary

Application in My Life

CHARACTER STUDY

PAGE ONE

"… considering the result of their conduct, imitate their faith." — Hebrews 13:7 NASB

Verse–Topic ____________________

Area of Study ______________________________

Key Scripture Passages ____________________________________

Record observations of life, insights of character, important events, relationship with God

Verse & Observations

Significant Observations of Character's Life

Major Character Qualities

Important Life Events

Relationship with God

Information from other Sources

Significant Principles Summary

Application in My Life

Character Study

PAGE ONE

"... considering the result of their conduct, imitate their faith." — Hebrews 13:7 NASB

Verse–Topic ____________________

Area of Study ______________________________

Key Scripture Passages ______________________________________

Record observations of life, insights of character, important events, relationship with God

Verse & Observations

Character Study

PAGE TWO

Significant Observations of Character's Life

Major Character Qualities

Important Life Events

Relationship with God

Information from other Sources

Significant Principles Summary

Application in My Life

CHARACTER STUDY

PAGE ONE

"... considering the result of their conduct, imitate their faith." — Hebrews 13:7 NASB

Verse–Topic ____________________

Area of Study ______________________________

Key Scripture Passages ______________________________________

Record observations of life, insights of character, important events, relationship with God

Verse & Observations

Significant Observations of Character's Life

Major Character Qualities

Important Life Events

Relationship with God

Information from other Sources

Significant Principles Summary

Application in My Life

Character Study

PAGE ONE

"… considering the result of their conduct, imitate their faith." — Hebrews 13:7 NASB

Verse–Topic ____________________

Area of Study ______________________________

Key Scripture Passages ____________________________________

Record observations of life, insights of character, important events, relationship with God

Verse & Observations

Significant Observations of Character's Life

Major Character Qualities

Important Life Events

Relationship with God

Information from other Sources

Significant Principles Summary

Application in My Life

Character Study

PAGE ONE

"... considering the result of their conduct, imitate their faith." — Hebrews 13:7 NASB

Verse–Topic ____________________

Area of Study ______________________________

Key Scripture Passages ______________________________________

Record observations of life, insights of character, important events, relationship with God

Verse & Observations

Significant Observations of Character's Life

Major Character Qualities

Important Life Events

Relationship with God

Information from other Sources

Significant Principles Summary

Application in My Life

Character Study

PAGE ONE

"... considering the result of their conduct, imitate their faith." — Hebrews 13:7 NASB

Verse–Topic ______________________

Area of Study ______________________________

Key Scripture Passages ______________________________________

Record observations of life, insights of character, important events, relationship with God

Verse & Observations

Significant Observations of Character's Life

Major Character Qualities

Important Life Events

Relationship with God

Information from other Sources

Significant Principles Summary

Application in My Life

Character Study

PAGE ONE

"… considering the result of their conduct, imitate their faith." — Hebrews 13:7 NASB

Verse–Topic ____________________

Area of Study ______________________________

Key Scripture Passages ____________________________________

Record observations of life, insights of character, important events, relationship with God

Verse & Observations

Significant Observations of Character's Life

Major Character Qualities

Important Life Events

Relationship with God

Information from other Sources

Significant Principles Summary

Application in My Life

Character Study

PAGE ONE

"... considering the result of their conduct, imitate their faith." — Hebrews 13:7 NASB

Verse–Topic ____________________

Area of Study ______________________________

Key Scripture Passages ____________________________________

Record observations of life, insights of character, important events, relationship with God

Verse & Observations

Significant Observations of Character's Life

Major Character Qualities

Important Life Events

Relationship with God

Information from other Sources

Significant Principles Summary

Application in My Life

Character Study

PAGE ONE

"... considering the result of their conduct, imitate their faith." — Hebrews 13:7 NASB

Verse–Topic ____________________

Area of Study ______________________________

Key Scripture Passages ____________________________________

Record observations of life, insights of character, important events, relationship with God

Verse & Observations

Significant Observations of Character's Life

Major Character Qualities

Important Life Events

Relationship with God

Information from other Sources

Significant Principles Summary

Application in My Life

Character Study

PAGE ONE

"... considering the result of their conduct, imitate their faith." — Hebrews 13:7 NASB

Verse–Topic ____________________

Area of Study ________________________________

Key Scripture Passages ______________________________________

Record observations of life, insights of character, important events, relationship with God

Verse & Observations

Significant Observations of Character's Life

Major Character Qualities

Important Life Events

Relationship with God

Information from other Sources

Significant Principles Summary

Application in My Life

Character Study

PAGE ONE

"... considering the result of their conduct, imitate their faith." — Hebrews 13:7 NASB

Verse–Topic ________________

Area of Study _________________________

Key Scripture Passages ______________________________

Record observations of life, insights of character, important events, relationship with God

Verse & Observations

Significant Observations of Character's Life

Major Character Qualities

Important Life Events

Relationship with God

Information from other Sources

Significant Principles Summary

Application in My Life

Character Study

PAGE ONE

"… considering the result of their conduct, imitate their faith." — Hebrews 13:7 NASB

Verse–Topic ________________

Area of Study __________________________

Key Scripture Passages ________________________________

Record observations of life, insights of character, important events, relationship with God

Verse & Observations

Significant Observations of Character's Life

Major Character Qualities

Important Life Events

Relationship with God

Information from other Sources

Significant Principles Summary

Application in My Life

Character Study

PAGE ONE

"… considering the result of their conduct, imitate their faith." — Hebrews 13:7 NASB

Verse–Topic ____________________

Area of Study ______________________________

Key Scripture Passages ____________________________________

Record observations of life, insights of character, important events, relationship with God

Verse & Observations

Significant Observations of Character's Life

Major Character Qualities

Important Life Events

Relationship with God

Information from other Sources

Significant Principles Summary

Application in My Life

CHARACTER STUDY

PAGE ONE

"... considering the result of their conduct, imitate their faith." — Hebrews 13:7 NASB

Verse–Topic ____________________

Area of Study ______________________________

Key Scripture Passages ____________________________________

Record observations of life, insights of character, important events, relationship with God

Verse & Observations

CHARACTER STUDY

PAGE TWO

Significant Observations of Character's Life

Major Character Qualities

Important Life Events

Relationship with God

Information from other Sources

Significant Principles Summary

Application in My Life

CHARACTER STUDY

PAGE ONE

"... considering the result of their conduct, imitate their faith." — Hebrews 13:7 NASB

Verse–Topic ____________________

Area of Study ________________________________

Key Scripture Passages ______________________________________

Record observations of life, insights of character, important events, relationship with God

Verse & Observations

CHARACTER STUDY

PAGE TWO

Significant Observations of Character's Life

Major Character Qualities

Important Life Events

Relationship with God

Information from other Sources

Significant Principles Summary

Application in My Life

DOCTRINE-ETHICS STUDY

PAGE ONE

"If you are asked about your Christian hope, always be ready to explain it." — 1 Peter 3:15 TLB

Doctrine–Ethic ________________________________

Record Scripture references related to selected doctrine/ethic & include insights gained from your study.

____

Reference

____

Reference

____

Reference

____

Reference

____

Reference

Doctrine–Ethic ______________________________

____
Reference

____
Reference

____
Reference

Additional Related Scripture References:

Word Definitions

Commentaries

Summarize Beliefs Related to Selected Doctrine-Ethic

Doctrine-Ethics Study

PAGE ONE

"If you are asked about your Christian hope, always be ready to explain it." — 1 Peter 3:15 TLB

Doctrine–Ethic ______________________

Record Scripture references related to selected doctrine/ethic & include insights gained from your study.

____

Reference

____

Reference

____

Reference

____

Reference

____

Reference

Doctrine–Ethic ______________________________

____
Reference

____
Reference

____
Reference

Additional Related Scripture References:

Word Definitions

Commentaries

Summarize Beliefs Related to Selected Doctrine-Ethic

DOCTRINE-ETHICS STUDY

PAGE ONE

"If you are asked about your Christian hope, always be ready to explain it." — 1 Peter 3:15 TLB

Doctrine–Ethic ______________________________

Record Scripture references related to selected doctrine/ethic & include insights gained from your study.

____

Reference

____

Reference

____

Reference

____

Reference

____

Reference

Doctrine–Ethic ______________________________

____
Reference

____
Reference

____
Reference

Additional Related Scripture References:

Word Definitions

Commentaries

Summarize Beliefs Related to Selected Doctrine-Ethic

Doctrine-Ethics Study

PAGE ONE

"If you are asked about your Christian hope, always be ready to explain it." — 1 Peter 3:15 TLB

Doctrine–Ethic ______________________________

Record Scripture references related to selected doctrine/ethic & include insights gained from your study.

____
Reference

____
Reference

____
Reference

____
Reference

____
Reference

DOCTRINE-ETHICS STUDY

PAGE TWO

Doctrine–Ethic ____________________

____
Reference

____
Reference

____
Reference

Additional Related Scripture References:

Word Definitions

Commentaries

Summarize Beliefs Related to Selected Doctrine-Ethic

DOCTRINE-ETHICS STUDY

PAGE ONE

"If you are asked about your Christian hope, always be ready to explain it." — 1 Peter 3:15 TLB

Doctrine–Ethic ______________________________

Record Scripture references related to selected doctrine/ethic & include insights gained from your study.

____
Reference

____
Reference

____
Reference

____
Reference

____
Reference

DOCTRINE-ETHICS STUDY

PAGE TWO

Doctrine–Ethic ______________________________

____
Reference

____
Reference

____
Reference

Additional Related Scripture References:

Word Definitions

Commentaries

Summarize Beliefs Related to Selected Doctrine-Ethic

DOCTRINE-ETHICS STUDY

PAGE ONE

"If you are asked about your Christian hope, always be ready to explain it." — 1 Peter 3:15 TLB

Doctrine–Ethic ______________________________

Record Scripture references related to selected doctrine/ethic & include insights gained from your study.

____

Reference

____

Reference

____

Reference

____

Reference

____

Reference

DOCTRINE-ETHICS STUDY

PAGE TWO

Doctrine–Ethic ______________________________

____
Reference

____
Reference

____
Reference

Additional Related Scripture References:

Word Definitions

Commentaries

Summarize Beliefs Related to Selected Doctrine-Ethic

DOCTRINE-ETHICS STUDY

PAGE ONE

"If you are asked about your Christian hope, always be ready to explain it." — 1 Peter 3:15 TLB

Doctrine–Ethic ______________________________

Record Scripture references related to selected doctrine/ethic & include insights gained from your study.

____

Reference

____

Reference

____

Reference

____

Reference

____

Reference

Doctrine–Ethic ______________________________

____
Reference

____
Reference

____
Reference

Additional Related Scripture References:

Word Definitions

Commentaries

Summarize Beliefs Related to Selected Doctrine-Ethic

Doctrine-Ethics Study

PAGE ONE

"If you are asked about your Christian hope, always be ready to explain it." — 1 Peter 3:15 TLB

Doctrine–Ethic ____________________

Record Scripture references related to selected doctrine/ethic & include insights gained from your study.

____

Reference

____

Reference

____

Reference

____

Reference

____

Reference

DOCTRINE-ETHICS STUDY

PAGE TWO

Doctrine–Ethic ______________________________

____
Reference

____
Reference

____
Reference

Additional Related Scripture References:

Word Definitions

Commentaries

Summarize Beliefs Related to Selected Doctrine-Ethic

DOCTRINE-ETHICS STUDY

PAGE ONE

"If you are asked about your Christian hope, always be ready to explain it." — 1 Peter 3:15 TLB

Doctrine–Ethic ______________________________

Record Scripture references related to selected doctrine/ethic & include insights gained from your study.

____

Reference

____

Reference

____

Reference

____

Reference

____

Reference

Doctrine–Ethic ______________________________

____
Reference

____
Reference

____
Reference

Additional Related Scripture References:

Word Definitions

Commentaries

Summarize Beliefs Related to Selected Doctrine-Ethic

DOCTRINE-ETHICS STUDY

PAGE ONE

"If you are asked about your Christian hope, always be ready to explain it." — 1 Peter 3:15 TLB

Doctrine–Ethic ____________________

Record Scripture references related to selected doctrine/ethic & include insights gained from your study.

____

Reference

____

Reference

____

Reference

____

Reference

____

Reference

DOCTRINE-ETHICS STUDY

PAGE TWO

Doctrine–Ethic ______________________________

____
Reference

____
Reference

____
Reference

Additional Related Scripture References:

Word Definitions

Commentaries

Summarize Beliefs Related to Selected Doctrine-Ethic

DOCTRINE-ETHICS STUDY

PAGE ONE

"If you are asked about your Christian hope, always be ready to explain it." — 1 Peter 3:15 TLB

Doctrine–Ethic ______________________________

Record Scripture references related to selected doctrine/ethic & include insights gained from your study.

____

Reference

____

Reference

____

Reference

____

Reference

____

Reference

Doctrine–Ethic ____

____

Reference

____

Reference

____

Reference

Additional Related Scripture References:

Word Definitions

Commentaries

Summarize Beliefs Related to Selected Doctrine-Ethic

Doctrine-Ethics Study

PAGE ONE

"If you are asked about your Christian hope, always be ready to explain it." — 1 Peter 3:15 TLB

Doctrine–Ethic ______________________________

Record Scripture references related to selected doctrine/ethic & include insights gained from your study.

____

Reference

____

Reference

____

Reference

____

Reference

____

Reference

DOCTRINE-ETHICS STUDY

PAGE TWO

Doctrine–Ethic ______________________________

____
Reference

____
Reference

____
Reference

Additional Related Scripture References:

Word Definitions

Commentaries

Summarize Beliefs Related to Selected Doctrine-Ethic

Doctrine-Ethics Study

PAGE ONE

"If you are asked about your Christian hope, always be ready to explain it." — 1 Peter 3:15 TLB

Doctrine–Ethic ____________________

Record Scripture references related to selected doctrine/ethic & include insights gained from your study.

____

Reference

____

Reference

____

Reference

____

Reference

____

Reference

Doctrine–Ethic ______________________________

____
Reference

____
Reference

____
Reference

Additional Related Scripture References:

Word Definitions

Commentaries

Summarize Beliefs Related to Selected Doctrine-Ethic

Doctrine-Ethics Study

PAGE ONE

"If you are asked about your Christian hope, always be ready to explain it." — 1 Peter 3:15 TLB

Doctrine–Ethic ______________________________

Record Scripture references related to selected doctrine/ethic & include insights gained from your study.

____
Reference

____
Reference

____
Reference

____
Reference

____
Reference

DOCTRINE-ETHICS STUDY

PAGE TWO

Doctrine–Ethic ____________________

____
Reference

____
Reference

____
Reference

Additional Related Scripture References:

Word Definitions

Commentaries

Summarize Beliefs Related to Selected Doctrine-Ethic

DOCTRINE-ETHICS STUDY

PAGE ONE

"If you are asked about your Christian hope, always be ready to explain it." — 1 Peter 3:15 TLB

Doctrine–Ethic ______________________________

Record Scripture references related to selected doctrine/ethic & include insights gained from your study.

____

Reference

____

Reference

____

Reference

____

Reference

____

Reference

DOCTRINE-ETHICS STUDY

PAGE TWO

Doctrine–Ethic ______________________________

____
Reference

____
Reference

____
Reference

Additional Related Scripture References:

Word Definitions

Commentaries

Summarize Beliefs Related to Selected Doctrine-Ethic

Doctrine-Ethics Study

Page One

"If you are asked about your Christian hope, always be ready to explain it." — 1 Peter 3:15 TLB

Doctrine–Ethic ______________________________

Record Scripture references related to selected doctrine/ethic & include insights gained from your study.

____

Reference

____

Reference

____

Reference

____

Reference

____

Reference

Doctrine–Ethic ______________________________

____
Reference

____
Reference

____
Reference

Additional Related Scripture References:

Word Definitions

Commentaries

Summarize Beliefs Related to Selected Doctrine-Ethic

DOCTRINE-ETHICS STUDY

PAGE ONE

"If you are asked about your Christian hope, always be ready to explain it." — 1 Peter 3:15 TLB

Doctrine–Ethic ______________________________

Record Scripture references related to selected doctrine/ethic & include insights gained from your study.

____

Reference

____

Reference

____

Reference

____

Reference

____

Reference

Doctrine–Ethic ____________________

____
Reference

____
Reference

____
Reference

Additional Related Scripture References:

Word Definitions

Commentaries

Summarize Beliefs Related to Selected Doctrine-Ethic

Doctrine-Ethics Study

PAGE ONE

"If you are asked about your Christian hope, always be ready to explain it." — 1 Peter 3:15 TLB

Doctrine–Ethic ____

Record Scripture references related to selected doctrine/ethic & include insights gained from your study.

____

Reference

____

Reference

____

Reference

____

Reference

____

Reference

DOCTRINE-ETHICS STUDY

PAGE TWO

Doctrine–Ethic ____________________________________

____

Reference

____

Reference

____

Reference

Additional Related Scripture References:

Word Definitions

Commentaries

Summarize Beliefs Related to Selected Doctrine-Ethic

DOCTRINE-ETHICS STUDY

PAGE ONE

"If you are asked about your Christian hope, always be ready to explain it." — 1 Peter 3:15 TLB

Doctrine–Ethic ______________________________

Record Scripture references related to selected doctrine/ethic & include insights gained from your study.

____
Reference

____
Reference

____
Reference

____
Reference

____
Reference

DOCTRINE-ETHICS STUDY

PAGE TWO

Doctrine–Ethic ______________________

____
Reference

____
Reference

____
Reference

Additional Related Scripture References:

Word Definitions

Commentaries

Summarize Beliefs Related to Selected Doctrine-Ethic

DOCTRINE-ETHICS STUDY

PAGE ONE

"If you are asked about your Christian hope, always be ready to explain it." — 1 Peter 3:15 TLB

Doctrine–Ethic ______________________________

Record Scripture references related to selected doctrine/ethic & include insights gained from your study.

____

Reference

____

Reference

____

Reference

____

Reference

____

Reference

DOCTRINE-ETHICS STUDY

PAGE TWO

Doctrine–Ethic ______________________________

____

Reference

____

Reference

____

Reference

Additional Related Scripture References:

Word Definitions

Commentaries

Summarize Beliefs Related to Selected Doctrine-Ethic

APPENDIX

About the Author

Catherine Martin is a summa cum laude graduate of Bethel Theological Seminary with a Master of Arts degree in Theological Studies. She is founder and president of Quiet Time Ministries, director of women's ministries at Southwest Community Church in Indian Wells, California, and adjunct faculty member of Biola University. She is the author of *Six Secrets to a Powerful Quiet Time, Knowing and Loving the Bible, Walking with the God Who Cares, Set my Heart on Fire, Trusting in the Names of God, Passionate Prayer, Quiet Time Moments for Women,* and *Drawing Strength from the Names of God* published by Harvest House Publishers, and *Pilgrimage of the Heart, Revive My Heart!* and *A Heart That Dances*, published by NavPress. She has also written *The Quiet Time Notebook, A Heart on Fire, A Heart to See Forever,* and *A Heart That Hopes in God*, published by Quiet Time Ministries. She is senior editor for *Enriching Your Quiet Time* quarterly magazine. As a popular speaker at retreats and conferences, Catherine challenges others to seek God and love Him with all of their heart, soul, mind, and strength. For more information about Catherine, visit www.quiettime.org.

About Quiet Time Ministries

Quiet Time Ministries is a nonprofit religious organization under Section 501(c)(3) of the Internal Revenue Code. Cash donations are tax deductible as charitable contributions. We count on prayerful donors like you, partners with Quiet Time Ministries pursuing our goals of the furtherance of the Gospel of Jesus Christ and teaching devotion to God and His Word. Visit us online at www.quiettime.org to view special funding opportunities and current ministry projects. Your prayerful donations bring countless project to life!

Quiet Time Ministries | P.O. Box 14007 | Palm Desert, California 92255
1.800.925.6458 | catherine@quiettime.org | www.quiettime.org

NOTES

INTRODUCTION

1. A.W. Tozer, *The Pursuit of God* (Harrisburg, PA: Christian Publications, 1948) pp. 9-10.
2. J.I. Packer, *Knowing God* (Downers Grove, IL: InterVarsity Press, 1973), p. 29.

CHAPTER 1 KnowingAndLoving

1. Howard Hendricks, Living by the Book (Chicago: Moody Press, 1991), p. 19.
2. Taken from The Challenge of Bible Translation by GLEN G. SCORGIE; MARK L. STRAUSS; STEVEN M. VOTH. Copyright © 2003 by Glen G. Scorgie, Mark L. Strauss, and Steven M. Voth. Used by permission of The Zondervan Corporation, pp. 20-21..
3. J. Robertson McQuilken, *Understanding and Applying the Bible* (Chicago: Moody Press, 1983), p. 69.
4. See Josh McDowell, *Guide to Understanding Your Bible* (San Bernardino, CA: Here's Life Publishers, 1982), p. 6..
5. Paul Enns, *The Moody Handbook of Theology* (Chicago: Moody Press, 1989), p. 160.
6. Ibid., p. 170.
7. Available online at www.iclnet.org/pub/resources/text/history/chicago.stm.txt.
8. Taken from Ancient Tab 2 Mod Trans by DAVID EWERT. Copyright © 1983 by The Zondervan Corporation. Used by permission of The zondervan Corporation. Pages 19-20.
9. Ibid., p. 186.
10. G.W. Bromiley, *The International Standard Bible Encyclopedia*, vol. 2 (Grand Rapids, Wm. B. Eerdmans, 2001), p. 114.
11. Ewert, p. 189.

CHAPTER 2 KnowingAndLoving

1. Merrill C. Tenney, *Galatians: The Charter of Christian Liberty* (Grand Rapids: Wm. B. Eerdmans Publishing Company, 1960), pp. 207-08.

CHAPTER 5 KnowingAndLoving

1. Amy Carmichael, "A Joy to Thee," in *Mountain Breezes* (Fort Washington, PA: Christian Literature Crusade, 1999), p. 182. Used by permission.
2. G. Campbell Morgan, *The Westminster Pulpit* (Grand Rapids: Baker Book House, 2006), vol. 8, p. 178.
3. Ibid., vol. 2, pp. 278-80.
4. Ibid., vol. 5, pp. 62-64.

A 30-DAY JOURNEY
KNOWING
& LOVING
THE BIBLE
Face to Face with God
in His Word
HOLY BIBLE
Foreword by
JOSH McDOWELL
CATHERINE MARTIN
Author of Six Secrets to a Powerful Quiet Time
KNOWING & LOVING THE BIBLE
MARTIN

CATHERINE MARTIN

Author of *Six Secrets To A Powerful Quiet Time*

THE QUIET TIME NOTEBOOK

The PRAYER Quiet Time Plan

THE QUIET TIME NOTEBOOK

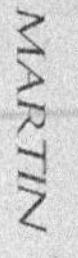

MARTIN

CATHERINE MARTIN

Author of *The Quiet Time Notebook*

THE QUIET TIME JOURNAL

Pouring Out Your Soul To The Lord

THE QUIET TIME JOURNAL

MARTIN

THE PASSIONATE PRAYER NOTEBOOK
MARTIN

CPSIA information can be obtained
at www.ICGtesting.com
Printed in the USA
FSOW04n1252280716
23206FS